Table of Contents

Introduction

There are moments in your life you never forget. One of these moments for me was the morning of my wedding. My soon-to-be wife texted to ask if I had cold feet. I told her I had warm socks and was not going anywhere. Another moment was when I watched the nurse put my baby girl, still a little blue, on my wife's chest after over 24 hours of labor. I will never forget my exhausted wife's facial expression; a combination of joy, disbelief, that our baby was finally here!

But then there are other moments. I'll never forget when my wife asked me if we would be okay. After months of stress and losing money in my new start-up dental office, I was depressed and burnt out. My wife knew I was struggling but did not know how dire the financial situation was. Every other time she'd asked, I had told her we were "fine." But this time, I looked her in the eyes, weak and defeated, and said, "Honey, I don't know anymore."

It was late November 2019. I had felt perpetually ill for weeks. I don't think I was sick, but I never felt good. I'd opened my dental office in April, and things had not gone as planned. By November, I had drained my savings and retirement, taking out working capital loans to make payroll twice. I spent each day trying to put on a strong, happy, optimistic face, but deep down, I was fraught with questions. Was I foolish to risk a stable, well-paying job to start an independent dental office? Did I listen to the right advice? Would I make it, or would my family suffer?

At the end of each work day, I re-calculated my runway—all the money and credit I had left to stay open. This included maxing all my high-interest credit cards and using a line of credit. I had six weeks left.

Six weeks until I would not make payroll, six weeks until it would all fall apart, six weeks until everyone would know I had failed. I started researching bankruptcy. Would I lose everything? My business? My home? What loans did I personally guarantee? What loans would I still need to pay?

This experience changed me. I became obsessed with understanding my numbers. It was not enough to *hope* each investment in my business would yield a positive return—I had to *know* it would. I had no margin for error; I could not afford to take any risks that would not pay off. Fear and anxiety could leave me stagnant and paralyzed, but that was no longer an option. I needed a consistent method of deciding what to prioritize in my business to increase profits with minimal risk.

I dug into every aspect of my business, from lab costs and materials to insurance participation and marketing. Nothing was off-limits. Eventually, I made the numbers work and found success in my business. I want to help you do the same.

This book is a collection of the strategies and tactics I implemented to improve my office. One primary approach was dropping out of as many PPOs as possible—but I had to do it strategically to maintain production. To avoid returning to that dark, hopeless place, I had to know I was bringing in enough treatment plans to keep my schedule productive.

Trust that I know that dropping a PPO can be scary. I know the fear and anxiety as the owner of a dental office that is running out of cash. But I also know what it is like to come out the other side of that struggle. This book is about creating a safe, predictable growth plan, and dropping out of PPOs is one of the best way to do that. I will show you how to drop a PPO with minimal fear and anxiety.

To learn the steps to drop a PPO, go to **page 61**. But if you want to know how to get *ready* to drop a PPO without losing your mind or spoiling your bottom line, please read the sections before that. I will provide you with the strategy and tactics needed to drop PPOs safely. This book is for dentists and dental office managers who are sick and tired of seeing 20% to 50% of their hard work literally written off by insurance companies in the form of adjustments.

Actual Profit Breakdown

To increase profit, you can improve two essential metrics: your profitability percentage and the volume of dollars going through your office. With a 65% overhead and 35% profit, you keep $0.35 on every dollar that enters your business. You can work to improve this percentage and take home more of every dollar you bring in. This could mean lowering overhead by paying off debt or finding less expensive lab and supplies vendors. It could also mean increasing your profitability by optimizing your current staff and equipment to generate more production, thereby increasing the number of dollars moving through your business.

Profit Amount and Overhead

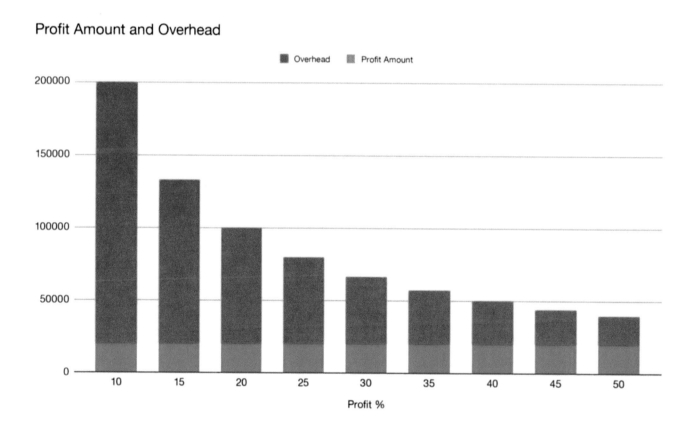

For example, a dental office with 65% overhead has a 35% profit margin. If the office collects $500,000, the owner will take home $175,000. If they want to take home $200,000 with the same 35% profit margin, they must increase their collection to $571,428.57. Or, they could still collect $500,000 but increase their profit margin to 40%, so overhead drops to 60%. Both of these methods lead to the same $25,000 increase in profits. These numbers get more extreme as your profit margins get smaller. A 10% profit on $1,000,000 equals a 20% profit on $500,000.

By looking at the profit chart on the previous page, you can see that a tiny profit margin requires massive production to reach the same goals. As the profit margin increases, the production needed to achieve the same profits drops significantly. You might think you have 35% profit margins, so this very thin profit illustration does not affect you. What if I told you your accurate production-based profit margins are closer to 16%?

On this page, you will find a pie chart demonstrating each expense category in a dental office. The pie chart shows a dental office's profit without debt service payments.

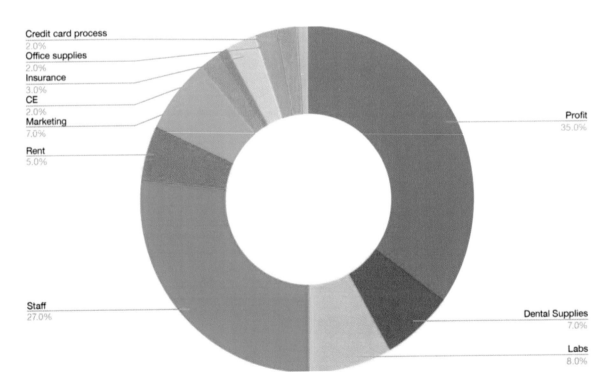

Many dentists say they have or aim for 65% overhead, but their actual overhead is much higher. When dentists talk about profit, they talk about EBITDA, which stands for earnings before interest taxes depreciation and amortization. This calculation excludes loan payments and taxes. A typical debt service payment is 5-7% of collections for many dentists. With another 7% of collections going out the door, overhead has increased to 72%, leaving you with only 28% profit.

I looked at the average collections for a solo doctor's office in America from 2000 to 2020. Using this data I created an expected collections rate for a dental office to be $712,901.

An office that collects $712,901 with 72% overhead ($513,288.72) only leaves $199,612.28 profit for the doctor.

Insurance Adjustments as a Marketing Expense

There is another often-overlooked category that I consider an expense in a dental office: agreements the dentist makes with other organizations that lower the dentist's effective fee. This can be seen in two major categories: insurance adjustments and finance charges from third-party financing companies.

This kind of expense is much more devious because it does not enter your business like other bills; it shows up as a decrease in revenue. Instead of collecting $1,000 for a crown, you only collect $700. This $300 difference is "just part of the business," but functionally, you would be in the same boat if you collected $1,000 and then paid $300 as an expense.

Many third-party financing options work similarly. Instead of collecting your full fee, you lose a percentage to the financing company. Again, you will not typically get a bill for this. You will see a decrease in revenue. These costs can be massive. My calculations will only assume a 40% write-off, but many offices can write off 50% of their production or more.

Including these insurance adjustments as an expense requires a little extra math because they impact both revenue and expense. This does not change the $196,812 end profit number but does decrease the percentages of the different expense categories. In other words, your profit slice is thinner but cut from a bigger pie. This might feel like a silly math exercise, but this breakdown of expenses is a far more accurate way of looking at our businesses.

To hit your $712,901 collection number with a 40% insurance adjustment, you must produce $1,188,168.33 of dentistry. $1,188,168.33 times 40% = $475,267.33 adjustment.

$712,901 in collections + $475,267.33 in adjustment = gross production $1,188,168.33

In this scenario, you collected $1,188,168.33 but paid an additional $475,267.33 in expenses as an insurance adjustment.

Our ending values
- Total full fee production: $1,188,168.33
- Total expenses with insurance adjustments as an expense: $988,556.05
- Total pre-tax profit: $199,612.28

Our new profit margins are 16.8%! We are still taking home the same $199,612.28, but it is a much thinner slice of a bigger pie. You might find this a little confusing at first. But remember, each of the expense categories represents the same dollar amount. This new 3% cost of rent (orange segment on the pie chart) is still $35,645.05 but instead of being 5% of $712,901 it is 3% of $1,188,168.33.

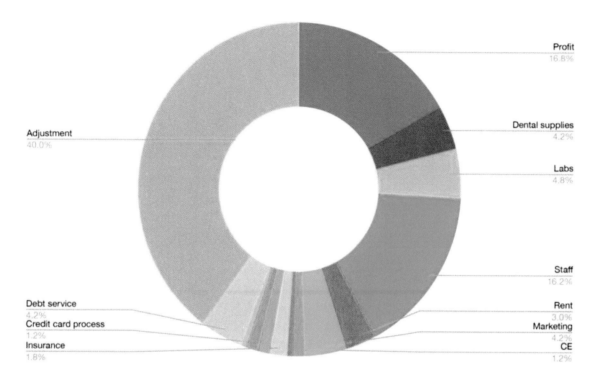

The thinner our profit margins are, the more difficult it is to run a business. A few no-shows can eat away your entire profit for the day. Since COVID, our supplies and labor costs have increased. The only thing that has yet to go up is insurance reimbursements. You most likely have raised your fees with your expenses, but if you are in network, you only increased your insurance adjustment slice; you have no control over your *reimbursement*.

An insurance adjustment is simply a marketing expense. I go in network in the hope of attracting and retaining patients. It is no different than other forms of marketing—mailers, Facebook ads, or sponsoring a local sports team. If you are in a network with a PPO, you are simply outsourcing your marketing to these different insurance companies.

In the above example, our insurance expenses are $475,267.33 per year. This is $39,605.61 a month. In my example, the office spends almost $40,000 monthly for this form of PPO marketing. How would you feel if your current marketing company started charging $40,000 a month?

There are some costs in your business you cannot cut. You must continue paying rent or your building loan. If you cut staff costs, you might lose your high-quality employees and be unable to replace them. If you use cheaper dental supplies, you will have more failures and need to redo work. If you use a cheaper lab, you might end up with an open margin or high restorations.

Dropping a PPO will not jeopardize your quality of care like cutting other expenses. Functionally, you're just firing an expensive marketing company. What is the negative side effect? Losing patients. So, all we need to do is find more cost-effective marketing methods to replace these patients.

In dental owner communities, there is a lot of fear surrounding losing patients due to abruptly dropping PPOs. This book aims to help you reduce your anxiety by creating an organized strategy for going out of network without going out of your mind.

The Standardized Dental Office

We need a baseline of understanding to effectively discuss net profit for patients or procedures. I created a "standardized dental office" to illustrate the numbers discussed throughout this book. This generic, solo doctor's office is a reference point for different calculations.

This calculation will help us determine a cost per chair time hour used to determine the net profit for a specific procedure. For this calculation, I separated procedure-specific costs such as lab or consumables; I calculated how many items I used for different procedures and assigned a dollar amount to each procedure. All non-direct procedure costs are treated as "time costs." The total time cost is divided by the total available chair time hours.

This four-operatory solo doctor's office works eight hours a day and four days a week.
- The collection: $712,901
- Office overhead: 65% of collections
- Debt service: 7% of collections
- Total overhead: 72% of collections

Procedure specific costs
- Lab: 8% of collections
- Material: 7% of collections

Time costs/Non-procedure-specific costs
- Chair time cost: 57% ($406,353.57)
- Total annual hours worked: 1,568 hours
- Cost to have the office open: $259.15 per hour
- Cost per operatory: $64.78 per hour

Schedule modifier

Despite your best efforts, you will not work your chair time at 100% capacity. No-shows, inclement weather, and sick employees inevitably prevent you from reaching your maximum potential, so I assume you only use 90% of your available chair times. This will increase your cost per chair time hour to $70.47.

Now that we know our chair time cost, we can look at the revenue generated from different procedures and use this data to determine the average profitability per procedure.

For revenue, I used my lowest and highest PPO for my zip code and my patients' most common fee schedule for the mid-level PPO. The cash fee was my zip code's average price for these procedures.

The following two graphs were created to illustrate net profit for a few different procedures. Then, we can divide by the number of chair time hours needed to complete this treatment. This method normalizes the data and allows for apples-to-apples comparisons between different procedures.

A few things should be clear after looking at these graphs. First, by treating patients with a better fee schedule, you can see a dramatic increase in profitability. The cost to perform each procedure is the same regardless of the fee schedule, so the fee schedule determines your profit margin.

Another thing to note is that profitability greatly increases when treatments are clustered together. This can be done by doing three fillings or three crowns in a single appointment. This requires a long stretch of continuous doctor time, so if your schedule is relatively full, you must pre-block time for this higher production and higher profit procedures. Extensive cases, such as full-mouth rehab, will be more profitable. You can see eight patients, each needing one crown or eight crowns. Both will result in the same total production and collection, but the eight separate patients take far more chair time and materials than doing eight units on one patient.

Profit Per Hour (Doctor)

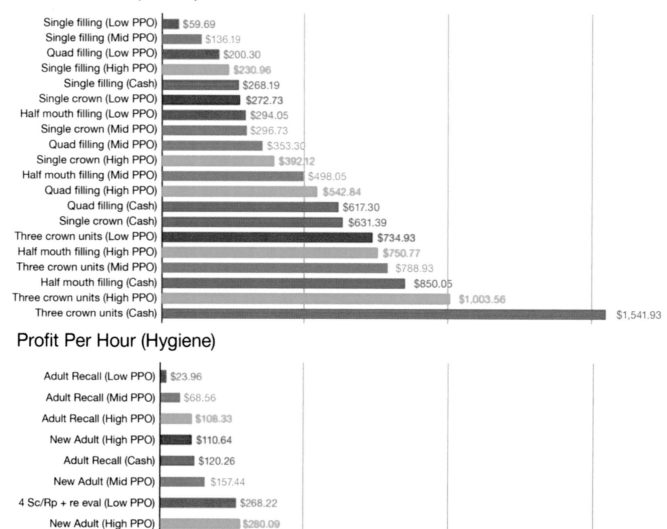

Profit Per Hour (Doctor):

- Single filling (Low PPO): $59.69
- Single filling (Mid PPO): $136.19
- Quad filling (Low PPO): $200.30
- Single filling (High PPO): $230.96
- Single filling (Cash): $268.19
- Single crown (Low PPO): $272.73
- Half mouth filling (Low PPO): $294.05
- Single crown (Mid PPO): $296.73
- Quad filling (Mid PPO): $353.30
- Single crown (High PPO): $392.12
- Half mouth filling (Mid PPO): $498.05
- Quad filling (High PPO): $542.84
- Quad filling (Cash): $617.30
- Single crown (Cash): $631.39
- Three crown units (Low PPO): $734.93
- Half mouth filling (High PPO): $750.77
- Three crown units (Mid PPO): $788.93
- Half mouth filling (Cash): $850.05
- Three crown units (High PPO): $1,003.56
- Three crown units (Cash): $1,541.93

Profit Per Hour (Hygiene)

Profit Per Hour (Hygiene):

- Adult Recall (Low PPO): $23.96
- Adult Recall (Mid PPO): $68.56
- Adult Recall (High PPO): $108.33
- New Adult (High PPO): $110.64
- Adult Recall (Cash): $120.26
- New Adult (Mid PPO): $157.44
- 4 Sc/Rp + re eval (Low PPO): $268.22
- New Adult (High PPO): $280.09
- 4 Sc/Rp + re eval (Mid PPO): $299.72
- New Adult (Cash): $319.44
- 4 Sc/Rp + re eval (High PPO): $415.23
- 4 Sc/Rp + re eval (Cash): $545.72

Although the hygiene appointments requires much less doctor time, the potential profitability per chair time hour dramatically decreases. In particular, the adult recalls for a low PPO have a profit margin of $23.96. If your schedule is full of low-profit recall appointments, consider dropping out of lower PPOs to make room for more high-value patients.

Consider how to increase average profitability per chair time hour to increase overall profitability. For the standardized dental office, we assume 1,568 total chair time hours in a year. We can use this information to determine how much net profit per chair time hour is needed to reach your profit goals.

- $100,000 = $63.78 profit per hour
- $200,000 = $127.78 profit per hour
- $300,000 = $191.33 profit per hour
- $400,000 = $255.10 profit per hour

If you want to increase your average profit per hour, you should spend more time at the bottom of these charts on page 11 and less at the top. Please note that an empty chair time hour costs you about $65, which will bring down your average. My goal is to help you achieve a consistent schedule that is about 90% full, allowing time for more high-value patients.

Recall Hygiene Appointments

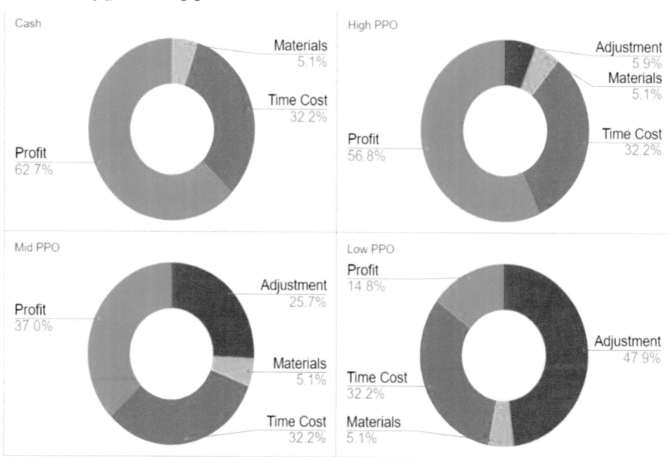

Don't confuse being busy with being productive. Being fully booked for recall might seem like a sign of solid business health, but depending on your patient and procedure mix, you could barely break even or only see a small profit.

A hygiene appointment has the highest risk of a no-show or last-minute cancellation. These appointments are relatively long compared to how much production is completed, so a no-show or last-minute cancellation has a relatively high time cost.

Hygiene recalls **profits decrease** as insurance **adjustments increase**. Unlike other types of appointments, the hygiene appointment is very time-intensive compared to its profitability. It may take very little doctor time, but the additional chair times can significantly impact your production capacity if you are in a chair-time-constrained office.

When there is a no-show or last-minute reschedule, you cannot fill, and no dental material is wasted, but you still incur time costs for operating your office. If a patient no-shows or cancels once, that time cost comes from your profits. This means the chair time cost is double when the patient comes in the second time for their appointment.

The double chair times could mean your effective net profit for that patient's appointment becomes negative. You can mitigate this problem by double-booking patients, which can lead to patients waiting or not being seen if everyone shows up. This might work out for a Medicaid mill or high-volume PPO office, but running on time can be a strong selling feature compared to the competition if you are trying to get more out-of-network patients.

Even if you have a high-paying PPO patient or a cash patient, you will not make any profit if they no-show you multiple times. Using up to 4-5 chair hours to do the exam and cleaning will not be profitable. You need to be mindful of patients who are chronically not showing up or canceling at the last minute.

Profit when a patient shows up on their first appointment:
- Cash: $125.96
- High PPO: $114.02
- Mid PPO: $74.25
- Low PPO: $29.65

Profit when a patient no-shows and reschedules (once):

- Cash: $61.18

- High PPO: $49.24

- Mid PPO: $9.47

- Low PPO: $ -35.13 (negative)

Goals, Strategies, and Tactics

One of the biggest mistakes dentists make in their business, myself included, is that we love to jump on a tactical plan. It feels good when we take action as a leader. But action is not always productive.

Before picking a tactic, set a strategy and ensure that the strategy aligns with your goals. If your goal is to make more money without working more hours, you could select many strategies to reach this goal. Cut expenses, expand to additional locations, or learn more profitable procedures. All of these are examples of paths to increase profits. However, if you pick a strategy and try to pair it with tactics that don't fit that strategy, you will have limited success.

Let's say your goal is to get from one side of a mountain to the other. The goal is the destination. The strategy is a general plan to get there. You could go straight to the summit and come back down, go around the mountain's edge, or dig a tunnel through the center. Which strategy is best? It depends. Going around the mountain's edge might be easier if you want to avoid the summit due to bad weather. Creating a tunnel might be the most intelligent strategy if you need to transport goods to and from your destination repeatedly; it will take more work upfront but will increase efficiency in the future.

Your tactics are the step-by-step tasks necessary to reach your goal. You will need very different tactics to reach the summit than to build the tunnel. Also, dividing your resources so half your people hike to the summit while the other half dig tunnels will slow down the overall progress for both.

You must set your destination (goal), choose a plan to get there (strategy), and then select your steps (tactics) that match well with your strategy.

Some might wonder why I am talking so much about topics other than dropping PPOs. I promise we will talk in great detail about dropping PPOs later in this book. But these topics will help you understand how to drop PPOs safely and conservatively. I like to think of it like this: If I was your coach and you wanted to train to run a marathon, you might think that all I would tell you to do is run. The end goal is to run a race successfully; focusing on running would make logical sense. But to improve your running, it makes sense to correct other specific things: I would ensure your stride is efficient and doesn't waste energy, and I would ensure you stretch correctly to decrease the risk of injury.

When my father first tried to run a marathon (26.2 miles), he was tired when he got to mile 21; most of his body was ready to finish except for one muscle, the anterior tibialis. This muscle is on the front of the shin and allows you to lift your foot. He had plenty of strength to push off and move forward, but he could not correctly lift his foot from the ankle joint. This ruined his running techniques and caused him to quit the race.

One small link in the chain would not work, causing the whole system to break down. Did my dad train for countless hours running? Of course. Did he stretch before every workout to increase mobility? He sure did. Did he train one small muscle on the front of his shin to help lift his foot? Nope.

With this book, I want you to increase the profitability of your practice. I understand you might want to get on the road and "start running" or dropping a PPO. But first, we will stretch and train. We work on some business muscle groups, so you always land on stable footing. These specific points of failure are called bottlenecks. In the next chapter, I will review these and how to find them.

Bottlenecks

When my office was losing money every month, I became obsessed with understanding my numbers. I had to make sure everything I did led to a positive ROI. After hours and hours of reading and researching, I returned to a book my father gave me back in high school.

My father recommended a book called <u>The Goal</u>, which introduced me to an idea that shaped how I see almost every decision in my business. This idea helped me target what needed to be done in my office. What was this powerful idea? The Theory Of Constraints.

The Theory Of Constraints took the business world by storm in 1984. It is taught in countless MBA and business schools and has guided manufacturing to increase efficiency and reduce waste. Though there is much detail to the theory of constraints, I will focus on a few key concepts:

1. **Your business is a series of dependent events. The input of one segment is the output of the next.**
2. **The tightest constraint or bottleneck in the system will control the final output of the entire system.**
3. **Expanding or improving the bottleneck or constraint will improve the output of the entire system.**
4. **A bottleneck is present when you see an accumulation of inputs that cannot all be processed into outputs.**
5. **Expanding the capacity of a non-bottleneck will not increase overall output, but it might increase overhead, leading to decreased profitability.**

These basic ideas seem simple but are incredibly impactful for almost every decision in your office. By targeting and improving the bottleneck, you can expand the capacity of your entire system, where the final output is profit.

I like to break down my business into two key phases: Treatment Plan Creation and Treatment Plan Absorption.

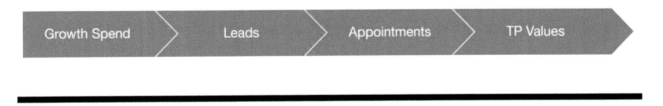

Treatment Plan Creation

This phase includes all the activities involved in generating a new treatment plan for new and existing patients. The steps are marketing spend, leads, appointments, and new treatment plans. Each step feeds into the next. Marketing generates leads. Lead generation creates appointments. An appointment should result in treatment plan formation. This can be visualized as water flowing through pipes: as the water exits one pipe, it enters the next.

Treatment Plan Absorption

This is the phase where we take out the accumulation of the treatment plan and convert it into collections. The accumulation of treatment plans is your treatment plan bank, which can be used to fill the schedule. The schedule will help us reach production goals. Completed production leads to collections. Decreasing friction around your bottleneck will allow liquidity to move through each segment more efficiently and quickly.

When setting your strategy for improving your office, we will examine three key bottlenecks on the chart and one input.

Bottleneck One: Accounts receivable

This bottleneck sits between production and collections. I typically like to keep A/R lower than the past 30 days' production.

Bottleneck Two: Treatment Plan Absorption Rate

This segment sits between your treatment plan bank and the schedule. We will look at two factors: First, how far out are you booked for treatment? Second, how much excess treatment plan value are you accumulating (patients who want to come in sooner but cannot be accommodated)?

Bottleneck Three: Total cost to attract a patient

Consider the cost to generate $1,000 in new treatment plan value. This cost includes direct marketing spend, insurance adjustment and financing write-offs, and discount write-offs. Some of these might not feel like marketing or sales expenses, but they are either direct or indirect costs that your business incurs to attract a patient or make it easier for them to agree to treatment.

Input: Sales and marketing input

Although this is not a bottleneck, it does act as your first input into the system. We want to see this number as low as possible but ensure you generate enough new treatment plans to reach your goals. This could mean dropping an insurance plan to reduce the insurance adjustment cost while increasing your direct marketing spend to compensate for the loss of those insurance patients.

Because each segment flows from one to the next, we first will make sure A/R is at an appropriate level. If it is, we can start moving back and working on correcting your treatment plan absorption rate. It is important to remember that as you fix one segment, it is not unusual to see a new bottleneck downstream because of the increased flow in the system.

A bottleneck is sometimes a good thing. For example, the surplus in the treatment plan may be in preparation for a significant expansion like equipping or another operatory. Going from two chairs to three is a 50% increase in chair time capacity. Having an enormous surplus of treatment plans and being booked for several months before adding the chair could be a good bottleneck. Or you might overspend on marketing to allow for a surplus of treatment plans before dropping a larger PPO. If you are expected to lose 10% of production when dropping a PPO but are booked out for three months, that potential loss in production will be mitigated.

Bottleneck One: Accounts Receivable

The bottleneck at A/R is the closest to your end of the line and the closest to you getting paid.

Now that we have targeted the problem, we must find the root cause. I like to write business SOAP notes (Subjective, Objective, Assessment, and Plan) to do this. Like a clinical SOAP note, we begin with the subjective finding and use that subjective information to determine which objective test we want to do. The result of these objective tests will lead to an assessment of the situation. This assessment will create our tactical plan of action.

For a patient, a SOAP note might look like this:

CC: Pain in the upper left

Subjective: The patient reports pain in the upper left for the past week.

Objective: Clinical exam shows healthy dentition and periodontium. Radiographs show no pathology in the dentition related to the pain.

Assessment: Pain seems unrelated to dental needs. This is a possible sinus infection or facial nerve pathology.

Plan: Refer to primary care physician to rule out other pathology.

I am sure when you started reading this SOAP note; you started picturing a bombed-out #14 causing the "pain on the upper left." We naturally reach for our most familiar tools to solve our problems. You might have heard the phrase, *to a hammer, every problem looks like a nail*. As dentists, with all of our clinical training, we believe that increased production will solve our financial problems. Your office might not have a clinical dental problem; it could have a marketing, management, or insurance participation problem.

A SOAP note for a business problem would be like this.

CC: I am producing more dentistry, but collections are not increasing.

Subjective: The office manager states all claims are being submitted on time.

Objective: A/R is three times the past 30 days of production. Reviewing old claims reveals multiple errors and missing information on claims that need to be re-submitted.

Assessment: Data is not being entered correctly when patients call in. Overall, production is not the problem.

Plan: Write up a new patient intake worksheet for all required data. Block off time at the end of the day to review the worksheets and patient charts so that the correct data is entered.

Create a plan of action that attacks the actual root cause of the problem. It's not always that someone is making a mistake—the person responsible could be working from false information, performing unnecessary steps, or being given too many tasks. In my own office, my office manager was overworked. I hired a second person to help with the schedule and take other related tasks off my office manager's plate. This allowed her to spend more time on the bottleneck task.

Digging Deeper into A/R

A high A/R number can have several causes, so we will need to dig into a few reports; the two I like to look at are "aging claims" and "delinquent accounts."

Aging claims show how old your claims are. If everything moves smoothly, a claim should be paid in 30-45 days. A claim can take longer if there is an error or the insurance needs a narrative. Insurance companies are incentivized to delay or avoid payment as much as possible.

Starting with aging claims makes looking at delinquent accounts much more manageable. Your delinquent accounts will be broken into a few categories:

- Current (0 to 30 days)
- Over 30 (31 to 60 days)
- Over 60 (61 to 90 days)
- Over 90 (91+ days)

Current: I don't stress about high current accounts. These are payments I expect to get later. A high current A/R could mean you recently had an excellent month and should have a higher-than-normal collection soon.

Over 30: I don't worry too much, but I do want my office manager to keep an eye on them. If there is a clear reason why the claim is not being paid.

Over 60: Realistically, a claim should only reach this level if something goes wrong or it seems a claim will not be paid as expected. The patient would have been sent an EOB by this time and should be aware of any outstanding balance.

Over 90: At this point, the insurance should have paid the claim. The patient could easily know this and not want to pay. If you have made multiple unsuccessful attempts to reach the patient, you should be sending them to collections. It has been my experience that less than 10% of bills sent to collections get paid. My policy is that patients sent to collections are dismissed from the practice.

Two scenarios can artificially increase A/R: secondary insurance and internal payment plans. If a patient has multiple insurances, you could wait for one claim to be denied and expect the secondary to pay. Patients feel that if they have two insurances, the second one will pay for whatever the first does not. This is not the case, and my policy is to collect all expected copay and deductibles according to the first insurance. If there is an overpayment, we refund the patient where appropriate.

Another scenario that will give you a misleading A/R is internal payment plans. This is where you, the dental office, allow the patient to pay in monthly installments. I am not a big fan of these payment plans because of the record-keeping and follow-up needed. I am trying to run a dental office, not a billing company. The only situation in which internal payment plans make sense is for Ortho. Because of the nature of ortho and the time it takes to get the final result, you have leverage if the patient fails to pay. On the other hand, if you are offering a payment plan for a crown and the patient stops payment, you cannot take the crown back.

These extended payment plans can inflate your over-90 A/R, depending on how they are managed. If you have a patient on a 12-month payment plan for ortho, you would walk out the total amount on the first appointment and subtract their payment every month when they pay. This puts them in the over 90-day category for nine months, but this is not necessarily a problem if they are active in treatment. By digging deeper into these A/R numbers, we can identify common problems, diagnose the cause, and prescribe a solution.

Examples:

- Errors during patient intake
- The patient provided the wrong insurance
- The patient thinks they have dental insurance when they only have medical
- Your front desk team is focused on making an appointment and not on collecting data
- Poor quality X-rays lead to rejection by the insurance company
- Poor charting documentation leads to insurance claims being denied

Solving these problems can be as simple as creating a worksheet or a better workflow to correct errors or remove an unnecessary step in the process. You may also find that additional staff is needed, or outsourcing some tasks would be beneficial. These are all things we want to address before moving on to our next bottleneck, Treatment Plan Absorption.

Bottleneck Two: Treatment Plan Absorption

After correcting accounts receivable, we can step back and start taking care of our treatment plan absorption phase. This bottleneck can be a little harder to see, but you'll notice that your schedule is overbooked and you have a large supply of treatment plans. This section will focus on how to optimize the schedule. If you are not getting booked out, this is not your bottleneck, and you need to move to the treatment plan formation stage and marketing input.

To engineer an optimal schedule, I like to focus on three goals:

1. Make sure the doctor is generating enough treatment plans to reach their treatment goals.
2. Prioritize appointments that lead to a higher level of production and collections.
3. Ensure the doctor is busy but not rushed; this ensures quality and prevents burnout.

To reach these goals, I have created a method called Hybrid Scheduling. This combines block scheduling, staggered scheduling, and the theory of constraints to create a better schedule.

Block Scheduling

You have probably heard about this type of schedule. This method blocks off time in the schedule for high-value appointments. These high-value appointments are called primary appointments. It tends to be longer production-heavy appointments requiring a long, continuous stretch of doctor time—for example, a large crown and bridge case.

There will also be appointments, such as small restorative care, that are considered secondary. Lastly, there will be non-productive appointments like crown cementation or a denture adjustment. These are tertiary appointments.

Prioritize large, more profitable appointments, then fill in the gaps in the schedule with the less-valuable secondary and tertiary ones. If there is an opening pre-blocked for primary treatment, you will not put lower-value appointments in that primary block. If you do, you will constantly fill the high-value time slots and never be able to book larger primary appointments. Put simply, you can fit two 30-minute appointments in a one-hour time slot, but you can't split a one-hour appointment into two separate 30-minute time slots.

A great way to visualize this is if you imagine you are trying to fill a jar. You have large rocks, small stones, and sand. If you want to fill the jar, you must put in the large rocks first, then the small stones, and lastly, the sand, which can fall into the tiny crevices. The large rocks will not fit in the jar if you first put in the small stones or the sand. Trying to shove everything into the jar this way will "break" the schedule. During your idle or slow time, you will feel anxious that you are losing money. Or you will be rushing around trying to make the schedule work, leaving you and your team feeling stressed and burnt out. A properly engineered schedule allows you to reach your production goals while working at a steady, deliberate pace.

The high-value blocks of time need to become sacred in the schedule. Low-value appointments can be put into these time slots only if they are still open 48 hours before the appointment time. A low-value appointment is, of course, better than an empty space in the schedule.

Staggered Scheduling

This form of schedule is less common than block scheduling. For most appointments, the patient is in the chair the whole time, but the dentist is not needed the entire time. You have room set-up, break-down, notes, walking the patient up, discussing payment, making a temp, or taking an impression. For all of these tasks, the dentist is not needed. The dentist is required for other tasks, such as prepping a tooth or an extraction. If you set two crown patients at 8:00 a.m., one will end up waiting. But if you time the second one to arrive at 8:45 a.m., the second patient can be prepped while the assistant finishes the temps for the first crown.

Staggered scheduling involves looking at when the doctor is needed for an appointment and planning overlap for when the doctor is busy in one room but not required in the next. Your schedule will look like zipper teeth or footsteps going down a path.

Theory of Constraints

This comes into play because we need a treatment plan before we have any treatment. To have a treatment plan, we must first have exams. Those low-production initial appointments are crucial to future production.

A bottleneck forms when one business segment cannot convert an input into an output. Having an overabundance of treatment plans will not only help you fill your schedule but will allow you to over-fill it. An over-filled schedule will allow you to focus on more profitable procedures, and patients will still sit at or near full capacity.

Hybrid Scheduling: Balancing Treatment Plan Creation and Absorption

Creating an ideal dental schedule is a tricky process of balancing many factors, and there are often trade-offs. When focusing on improving just one thing, it often ends up hurting something else.

I wanted to understand better how many new treatment plans I would need to reach my production goals. For this, I looked at three basic types of appointments:

- New Patients
- Recalls
- Production (fillings, crowns, extractions, etc.)

On average, a new patient appointment will generate a small amount of production but a larger treatment plan. A recall will generate roughly the same amount of production as a new patient but a smaller treatment plan. A production appointment will create more production per hour and consume an equal amount of treatment plan value. To help you visualize these concepts, I want to assign some value to each appointment.

- The new patient generates $150 in production and $1,000 in treatment plan value.
- The recall appointment generates $150 in production and $400 in treatment plan value.
- The production appointment generates $500 in production and a $500 negative treatment plan (the treatment plan value is negative because you will be removing this treatment plan when you create this production).

For this office, we assume a solo doctor's office with four operatories, working eight hours a day, four days a week.

Total chair time hours = 4 chairs x 8 hours x 4 days x 4 weeks in a month = 512 total chair time hours per month. This number is the maximum available chair time to see patients.

This office gets 50 new patients monthly for this example. These new patients generate the same production as the recall but a much larger treatment plan value. For this reason, the office will want to schedule all 50 of these new patients automatically.

If each new patient appointment takes an hour, it will generate $1,000 in treatment plan value and $150 in production. This also consumes 50 of our total chair time hours, leaving us with 462 chair time hours left for the month.

Starting, the office will have generated $50,000 in new treatment plan value and $7,500 in production from these new patient exams. To determine a good balance between production appointments and recalls, the office must chart how each production and recall hour affects the production and treatment plan totals. The chart on the next page represents how the remaining 462 hours of chair time are scheduled. On the left, the office has 462 hours devoted to production and 0 hours devoted to recalls. As you move right, the office devotes less time to production and more time to recalls.

The x-axis of the chart represents the additional chair time hour used for recalls or production. On the left, all additional chair time hours after the 50 new patients are devoted to production. As you shift from left to right, additional chair time is taken from production but given to recalls for treatment plan formation. The blue line represents the maximum production you will have given your current chair time usage. The red line represents the treatment plan formation rate. If the treatment formation rate is negative, you consume treatment plans faster than you create them. If the treatment value exceeds zero, you create treatment plans faster than you can consume them.

Understanding Production Equilibrium

The chart's red line represents treatment plan formation as you see more recalls. The blue shows total production decrease as less time is devoted to production appointments.

If you focus on the far left of the graph, you will get the maximum production number, but you will be draining away your treatment plans. Also, to achieve this schedule, the doctor must perform procedures in four operatories simultaneously.

As you go from left to right, the red line crosses the x-axis. This is when you generate enough treatment plans to hit your maximum production number. I consider this the Production Equilibrium, where you create treatment plans as fast as you consume them.

Final production and Final treatment plan

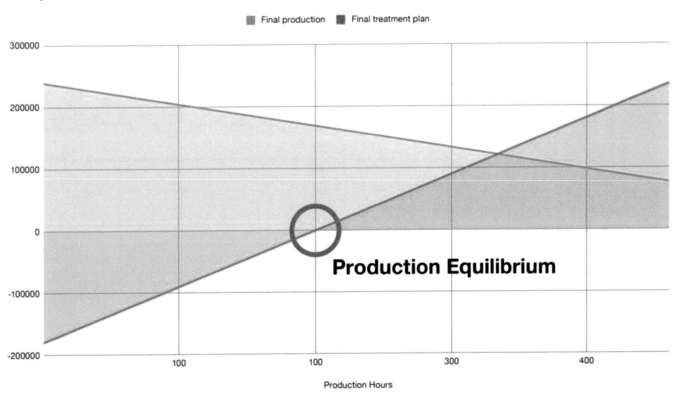

Insight From the Graph

If you stay precisely at this Production Equilibrium Point, you will maximize your current production but might undercut your future success.

As you shift right, you will generate more treatment plans than you can handle. This will cause a supply and demand imbalance in your schedule. This will allow you to do a few things:

1. If you have a 20% surplus of treatment plans, you can focus on the top 80%—the most productive treatment plans and procedures.
2. By creating a surplus of treatment plans, you can safely drop out of some PPOs. Even if you lose patients, you still have enough treatment plans to keep you busy.
3. With these excess treatment plans, you can increase your capacity by adding chairs or employees.

How to Increase Treatment Plan Formation at a Faster Rate

There are other ways to increase treatment plan values. An increase in effective marketing will cause an increase in new patient flow (a new patient typically has a larger treatment plan than existing patients). Additionally, you can increase the average new treatment plan value by learning new procedures that you are currently referring out, such as ortho or endo. Finally, consider adding new procedures you are not referring, such as sleep treatment or Botox. If done well, and you can learn to market and sell these procedures effectively, your treatment plans and production values will increase.

As you shift further to the right of this chart, you will sacrifice short-term cash flow for longer-term price increases. This long-term profitability growth will trigger increased cash flow in the future.

Times Tables

Now that we understand the profitability of each procedure and know we should generate enough treatment plans to keep the schedule at least 90% full, we want to keep our patients and doctors happy by creating a schedule that will not double-book the doctor.

It might seem simplest to just schedule without a plan, but this will lead to a few negative outcomes:

- Patients will end up waiting and be unhappy
- Planned treatment will not be done because the doctor is not available
- Appointments will be artificially lengthened to allow the doctor to be available

To construct a times table, you'll first need to create a succinct table for each procedure. Record the "chair time" required for an appointment in one column. "Chair time" refers to the total duration the chair is occupied, encompassing activities such as note-taking or making impressions, even if the doctor's presence isn't required. The subsequent column should indicate when the doctor's involvement is essential. It's crucial to accurately allocate the doctor's time based on when they are genuinely needed. Think of these tables as puzzle pieces designed to optimize your schedule, ensuring it remains fully booked while minimizing instances of double-booking the doctor.

Are You a Doctor-constrained Or a Chair-constrained Office?

A Times Table is only valuable if doctor time is your constraining variable. This means that the doctor's availability is holding back the schedule. There are a few ways to correct this. First, use times tables to optimize the doctor's time. Second, delegate as many nonclinical tasks as possible so the doctor's time is spent on the highest-value task. These could be tasks like putting in payroll or submitting an order.

If you have a doctor-constrained office, you will see that the doctor is constantly busy while other support staff are waiting. If, on the other hand, the doctor has idle time while chairs sit empty or there are other holes in the schedule, you do not have a doctor-constrained office.

Looking at the tables (on the next page), it takes an hour of chair time to do a quad filling, but the dentist is only needed for 40 minutes of the time. The first ten minutes are for seating the patient, and the last ten minutes are for walking the patient up, turning over the room, and writing notes.

If you had a full day of quad fillings, you would stack them offset from each other so these appointments overlap slightly. The doctor would work steadily all day without wasting time between appointments, but he/she would not be double booked.

It can be helpful to set some example schedules on a sheet of paper and then mark down where the doctor must be. You will most likely find that at some times, the doctor is double booked and people are waiting, while at other times, the doctor is idle and not needed.

You can increase production by allowing small, strategic gaps in the schedule. To do this, I like to make a "Times Table" for different procedures. These simple tables show when a chair is utilized and when the doctor is needed. This will allow the scheduler to stagger appointments so the doctor is not double booked.

Single Filling

Time	Chair	Doctor
00	▓ (chair)	
10	▓ (chair)	█ (doctor)
20	▓ (chair)	█ (doctor)
30	▓ (chair)	
40		
50		

Quad Filling

Time	Chair	Doctor
00	▓ (chair)	
10	▓ (chair)	█ (doctor)
20	▓ (chair)	█ (doctor)
30	▓ (chair)	█ (doctor)
40	▓ (chair)	█ (doctor)
50	▓ (chair)	

Crown Prep

Time	Chair	Doctor
00	▓ (chair)	
10	▓ (chair)	█ (doctor)
20	▓ (chair)	█ (doctor)
30	▓ (chair)	█ (doctor)
40	▓ (chair)	█ (doctor)
50	▓ (chair)	

Crown Cement

Time	Chair	Doctor
00	▓ (chair)	
10	▓ (chair)	█ (doctor)
20	▓ (chair)	
30		
40		
50		

Recall

Time	Chair	Doctor
00	▓ (chair)	
10	▓ (chair)	
20	▓ (chair)	
30	▓ (chair)	
40	▓ (chair)	
50	▓ (chair)	█ (doctor)

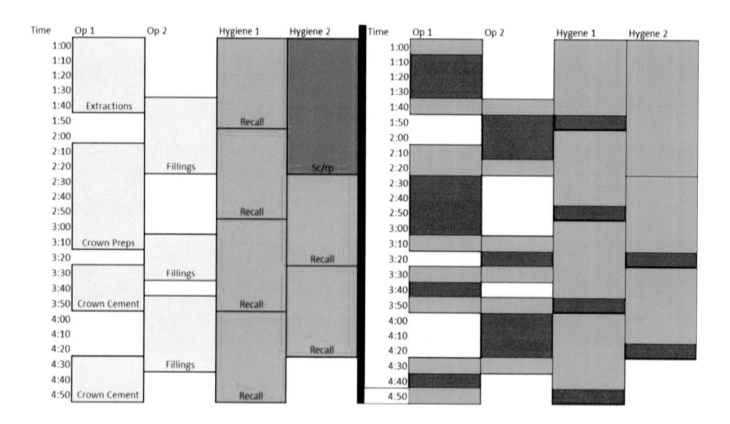

The above schedule is based on staggered scheduling and the Times Tables. On the left, it might look like there is a lot of unused chair time. But if we look at where the red doctor time is on the right, we can see that the doctor would be fairly consistent throughout the day with very little idle time (1:40, 2:20, 3:10, and 4:30) and very little time when the doctor is double-booked (1:50, 2:50, 3:20, and 4:20). This allows for a smooth, consistent, and productive day.

If the person/people creating the schedule do not have a clinical background, it is crucial that they at least understand when different resources are needed.

Scheduling SOAP Note

CC: The doctor is always behind and stressed out.

Subjective: The doctor is burnt out and running behind schedule.

Objective: Appointments are put in any opening, regardless of whether you have the staff or doctor time to see them.

Assessment: The schedule is not being planned based on available resources.

Plan: Train the assistant so the doctor can better delegate tasks such as making temps. Review the tasks the doctor is doing and see what can be delegated, such as ordering supplies. Create Times Tables for all appointments so the scheduler knows when the doctor is available.

Consistently Re-Check Bottlenecks

If you have been correcting your treatment plan absorption phase for the past few weeks, you might have noticed a problem with A/R. This could be because you are producing more dentistry with your newly optimized schedule, which means more claims and payments going to your front desk.

Bottleneck formation like this is normal and even expected. Remember, if a bottleneck is corrected, pressure will be released. The increase in flow through the system can trigger a new bottleneck further down. Let's say your previous methods would allow you to deal with $50,000 a month in production, but because you're now producing $75,000, your old system and capacity need to catch up. It would be best to revisit your A/R plan to make it more efficient or add staff to increase capacity.

Five-Year Net Profit

In the chart on the next page, we look at each insurance plan's net profit. For all patients, we assume that they are coming in for their regular recalls and that the other treatment, such as crowns and fillings, is in addition to preventative treatment.

Unsurprisingly, the more operative you do, the more profitable the patient will be. It is also evident that you become more profitable as you move from low to mid to high PPO. The exciting thing is that because your baseline cost to treat each of these patients is the same, the difference in profitability increases dramatically as your reimbursement increases. **A 16.8% increase in fee from the example earlier in this book can double profitability because that additional money does not go to additional overhead; it can go straight into your pocket.**

This data can be used to help evaluate how much you can do to attract these patients. Spending $300 to attract a low-PPO recall patient that will generate $236.10 would not be a wise business decision. On the other hand, spending $500 to attract a high PPO patient who needs one crown ($1,681.35 profit) gives you a profit margin greater than three to one.

Looking at a metric like new patient numbers alone can be misleading. I like to look at expected production. For example, say one office spends $5,000 to send out mailers, which attracts ten high PPO patients who need a quad of fillings. Another office spends $5,000 to attract 20 low-PPOs who all need a single crown. Who is more successful in this case?

In the scenario above, you would have a profit of $16,350.10 or a final net profit of $11,350.10 after paying for the mailers for the ten high PPO patients. In attracting the 20 low PPO patients who need a crown, your expected net profit will be $13,623.80, and after you pay for the mailer, you are left with $8,623.80. In this example, by attracting the ten high PPO patients vs. the 20 low PPO patients, you would have $2,726.30 (31.61%) more profit. In addition to that, you would need fewer chair time hours to take care of the ten filling patients compared to the 20 crown patients.

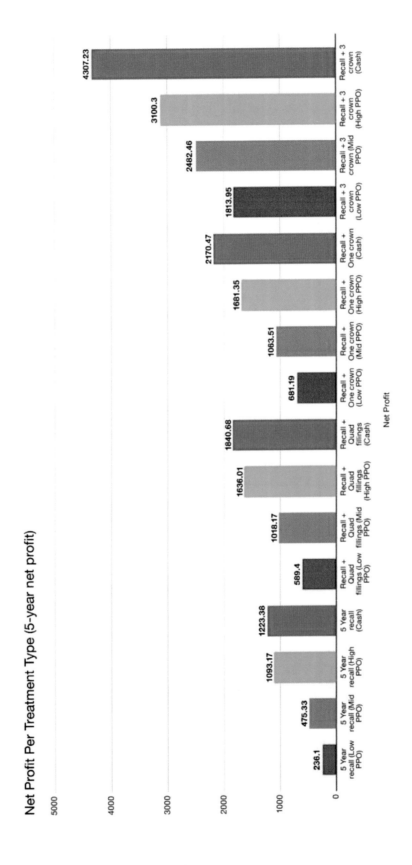

Net Profit Per Treatment Type (5-year net profit)

Five-Year Net Profit SOAP Note

CC: I need more new patients so that I can make more money.

Subjective: New patient numbers "feel" low compared to what doctors think other dental offices are getting

Objective: The doctor's schedule is booked for two weeks, and hygiene cannot get a new patient in for three months. When a new patient calls, they are being put on the waiting list. This office is also in network with many insurance plans with a write-off ranging from 20 to 50% of the office's full fee.

Assessment: The office is doing a sufficient amount of marketing to attract new patient phone calls, but many people are not scheduling because they are unwilling to wait three months for an appointment. This office is also in network with multiple plans, some paying much worse than others.

Plan: Figure out which insurance plan is paying on the lowest overall fee schedule. Then, work on a plan to start dropping the lowest-paying plans. Even if this office does lose a percentage of its patients, they will still be booked out, and the doctor should expect to keep a full schedule. This office will also start pre-booking time for new patients and emergencies. This will allow them to attract more patients who are more profitable. An additional assessment will need to be done in three to six months to determine if additional plans can/ should be dropped at that time.

Bottleneck 3: Treatment Plan Creation

Once you have corrected your A/R and optimized your schedule for a better flow, it's time to consider the cost of generating new treatment plans. The metric I will use for this is the total cost to generate $1,000 in "acceptable" treatment plan value. The "acceptable" treatment plan is one that you think has a relatively high chance of being accepted by the patient. You can inflate these numbers by creating unrealistic treatment plans for the patient's budget or desires, which benefits no one in the long run.

The total cost is all your direct costs, such as ad spend, insurance adjustments, and revenue lost from third-party financing. I consider all three of these as sales and marketing costs.

Marketing includes any activity or expense that attracts a lead to your office. Sales activities are any action or expense that moves the lead to make a financial or time commitment to your office; that commitment could be for a consult or treatment.

Dentists are going in-network for two reasons: to attract leads or potential patients (marketing) and to make it easier to convert these patients to treatment due to a lower out-of-pocket expense (sales). Third-party financing acts primarily in the realm of helping you sell a case by allowing the patient to break up their treatment into smaller payments.

Before discussing reducing the cost to generate $1,000 in acceptable treatment plans, our first call is to ensure we generate enough additional treatment plan value to reach our production goals. Cutting down on marketing spend can be counterproductive if it leaves you with idle chair time. Always remember your chair times: whether you have a patient or not, the cost must be paid.

Selling Larger Treatment Plans

A few methods exist to increase your average treatment plan size without being unethical.

Provide a more comprehensive treatment plan. Adding these services by learning skills such as TMJ treatment or ortho can expand the potential treatment plan value.

Keep more treatment in-house. By expanding your skill set so you are not referring out implant placement or molar endo, you can add those referred treatment plan values to your treatment plan bank. The one really good thing about this is that you can track, on average, how many of these cases get referred out and completed by the patient, which means you can confidently predict how keeping this treatment in-house would impact your treatment plan value.

Addressing All Non-Financial Concerns

Before any discussion about money can start, two other important questions must be answered in the patient's mind. First, will the patient be able to get the desired result? And second, will the patient have a treatment experience that meets their expectations? Discussing money will be difficult if you do not first satisfy these needs.

Addressing these two areas of concern allows you to address financial issues without distractions. This will limit the non-committal answers like "I don't know" or "I need to speak with my husband or wife." These wishy-washy statements, although sometimes legitimate, are often stalling techniques.

Learning to Sell Without Being Sales-y

The key to selling dental treatments without feeling like you're becoming that grimy, sales-y person is to uncover the patient's core emotional drives. Find out why the patient desires your services, then connect that to the benefits your services provide.

I don't know if it is because I have a bachelor's degree in psychology or because I enjoy socializing, but I genuinely enjoy speaking with patients about their wants and needs. I don't use a script or sneaky methods like Neuro-Linguistic Programming (NLP) to trick people into saying yes. I just have some methods and philosophies I use to help uncover their needs to serve them better.

As clinicians, we typically sell the process because we are trained to focus on that. We talk about how long and what steps will be needed to complete a task.

On the other hand, a patient buys the result, like the young professional who wants to fill that gap between 8 and 9 that they've felt self-conscious about since middle school or the grandma whose denture flips over like an Olympic gymnast every time she talks. These people don't want more porcelain or plastic in their mouths. They want to feel more comfortable and confident.

The line between our processes happening and their result being achieved is typically the price. But you, as the clinician, and they, as the patient, look at this from extremely different perspectives. It's like having a painting you made sitting between you and the patient. You see the back of it, all the hard work and thought you put in to make it materialize into a fantastic piece of art. On the other hand, the patient looking at the front of the painting sees something completely different. He sees an old man fishing with his adult son. The image reminds him of fishing with his father, who passed away two years ago. You see the pieces and process. They see the result.

Why do we love to buy but hate to be sold? It's all about how much value is gained compared to what is given. On a strictly business level, you gain value by providing a service for a price greater than your costs. The patient gains value when your services are worth more to them than the price they pay.

A patient probably isn't going to walk in and tell you what their core emotional drivers are. Luckily, we are all trained extensively in diagnosis. We know how to pull facts about a patient's medical history and connect the dots to see if they are a good candidate for the type of treatment we offer. We can use those same diagnostic questioning skills to uncover their other needs.

You want to ask directed but open-ended questions that help discover the patient's wants and needs. Then, let them talk and fully listen. What are their pain points? Are they happy with their smile? Are they scared of treatment? Do they have time constraints? Are they worried about working a payment into their budget? Not every objection you hear is directly about your price. By uncovering their needs, you can find ways to fill them.

Breaking Down Large Lump Sums Into a Monthly Payment

When talking about financing options with a patient, you want to make sure you can cover three key factors:

- You have already addressed all non-financial concerns.
- You can break down a larger sum payment into smaller payments through third party financing options.
- You can help the patient find opportunities in their budget to afford your treatment.

Most people don't budget for surprise expenses. This is why many patients who see $1,200 for some restorative work can feel like it is out of their reach. But a $100 monthly payment could be very accessible.

Many dental offices work with third-party financing companies. Care Credit is a company I use. They have fast approvals, and many patients already have an account. Another bonus is that I am paid upfront, even if the payment plan allows the patient to make payments for a year or more. As a start-up, this is very important for cash flow reasons. These third-party financing companies have costs similar to insurance adjustment—they are subtracted from the payment. But, I would much rather lose 10-15% of my fee to a financing company than 40% to an insurance company.

A $1,200 lump sum can become a $100 monthly payment with something like Care Credit. Because most people pay their other bills every month, adding $100 to their monthly budget is relatively easy.

Finding Ways to Work Your Treatment Into Your Patient's Budget

Whenever we want to spend more, it would be great to boost our income to take care of all our spending. Sadly, when we take on expenses, we must remove something else to work this new payment into our budget.

We often spend money on things that don't add much value to our lives. An impulse buy can leave you with buyer's remorse or an overpriced coffee that gives 10 minutes of enjoyment at best. These low-value spending habits don't improve your patient's quality of life as much as the long-term benefits of restoring oral health.

When talking to the patient about their budget, it is essential to help them see how much can be diverted from other areas so they can spend the same each month but enjoy increased value and quality of life. That same $100 a month equals less than $3.34 a day. By helping your patient understand how they can omit short-term or low-value purchases from their budget, you can help them afford your services without a dramatic sacrifice or increase in income.

It is important that when you make these budget swap comparisons, you discuss unnecessary expenses like eating out, luxury goods, or travel. You want to avoid comparing your services to necessary payments like rent or car payments. These are high-value necessities for most people. Your goal is to have your patient shift money from lower-value spending to your higher-value services.

Re-Check Your Other Bottlenecks

Now that you have increased your acceptable treatment plan formation, you might notice that your schedule or A/R has some capacity issues as more production flows through the system. Check back in on these other bottlenecks before you make any more changes.

Reducing Your Marketing Expenses

We are getting very close to discussing dropping PPOs. Remember, I treat an insurance adjustment like a marketing expense, so every time we drop a PPO, we effectively decrease our marketing budget. Before we go too deep into reducing our marketing expenses, we will review a few types of marketing so we can discuss the pros and cons of different methods.

Marketing Methods

Internal and external marketing

Internal marketing uses your current patient base to attract new patients. This could be anything from asking for referrals or asking for Google reviews.

External marketing

When you first think of marketing, you most likely visualize this. This is an activity designed to attract patients into your practice. After you have attracted an external patient and they come into the practice, you use internal marketing to maximize your value from that patient.

Intent–based marketing

This is used when the patient is actively searching for a service you provide. The most common form of this is a Google search. A patient might search for something like "dentist near me" or "to fix a cracked tooth." This patient has a clear need and desire for services. The problem with intent-based marketing is that we cannot control the patients' demographics or purchasing power.

Interruption-based marketing

This form of marketing is sent to a group of potential patients with similar characteristics. This might be a geographic area (within 20 miles of your office), income level, if they recently moved, life events (like a marriage or divorce), or other characteristics. You can at least partially target a group you feel would be a good fit for your office. This can be very helpful for targeting people for specific high-end services such as clear aligners or implants. Though you can control the demographics, you cannot control actual desire. Because of this, you might need to reach out to many people to find only a handful interested in your offer.

Marketing Crash-Course Glossary

Lead: Someone who has reached out with interest in your practice or services but has yet to commit financially or with their time.

Marketing: Any money or time spent to attract a lead.

Sales: Any money or time spent to convert the lead into making a financial or time commitment.

Value: The subjective interpretation of how useful, desirable, or urgent a product or service is for the end user.

Cost: Any resources or unpleasantness that will detract from the product or service's value. This could be money, time, or an unpleasant experience.

PPO participation: I have said this before and will say it again. You outsource your marketing to an insurance company when you are in their network. The insurance company might be doing Facebook ads or sponsoring a stadium; it is all marketing to attract patients.

Remember, patients don't want dental insurance. They want the benefits that good dentistry provides. You, the dentist, provide the benefits they are seeking. Dental insurance is just a vehicle patients feel will help them get quality treatment cost-effectively.

Ground marketing: Any activity involving face-to-face community contact. This could be a paid live event like getting a table at a wedding convention or a free event like visiting a school and presenting on oral health. This would also include speaking to other dentists for referrals. Whenever the local oral surgeon or orthodontist comes into your office for a chat, they are ground marketing.

This form of marketing is cheap but can be time-consuming. It tends to increase the chances of the patient showing up; you build trust through your face-to-face connection. There is a reason why all your dental material sales reps will pop in randomly or offer a lunch and learn.

Ground marketing can be considered a form of external interruption marketing. You are pulling patients from outside your office, and they can be targeted based on common characteristics. For example, setting up a table at a wedding convention can be very beneficial if you are looking for cosmetic, ortho, or whitening cases. On the other hand, if you are trying to find families with children, you might target a parenting expo.

Mailers: Just like it sounds, you send a mailed postcard to a group of people. Like ground marketing, this can be highly selective based on the geographic area and other demographics like age, number of people in the home, or income level.

SEO: Stands for search engine optimization. This will determine where you rank on the SERP (search engine results page). The best thing about SEO is also the worst: it is tough to manipulate Google to rank quickly. This creates stability and predictability but requires more time and money before seeing an increase in page rank, leading to more new patients.

Although a marketing company should do most SEO, you can supplement to help boost your ranking. This could mean additional blog content you and your team wrote, guest blogging to attract backlinks, or creating a YouTube channel that links back to the website.

Local SEO: This will primarily be your Google My Business page. You can think of this as a mini website on the search page and Google Maps. This is very high-value real estate for people searching for a dentist.

To improve your rank, follow these steps:

- Ask for Google reviews. Having a high volume of positive Google reviews will greatly help your ranking.
- Specifically, ask the patient to write a little about their experience. This provides social proof: if someone starts reading through your reviews and sees other patients saying something great about you on top of a 5-star review, you will increase your chances of success. Also, when the patient writes something, they will most likely use keywords that can pop up in search, such as "crown," "veneer," or "braces." If someone searches for something like "dentist to fix broken crown," you will increase your odds of showing up higher on the ranking.
- **Respond to reviews:** If you get a good review, respond with a thank you. In your response, you do not need to worry about putting in keywords; it will not improve your ranking. I also suggest responding to negative reviews. My main goal is not to get the review taken down but to have something for another future patient to read to defend our position.

Google PPC: paying Google to rank your page higher on the search results. Google PPC is bold on the top of the search page and says "sponsored." These links are paid per click so that they can be expensive. However, because this is an intent-based marketing source, you can be confident that there is some interest and even urgency from the patient. This means they will likely have a strong interest or desire for what they are searching for.

Ads on Facebook/ Instagram/ TikTok are examples of interruption-based marketing. Facebook has a massive amount of data on its users, so selecting people based on particular demographics is easy. The problem here is that people are not on these platforms to search for dentists, so they are not in a buying frame of mind for your services. Like all marketing, you can get a positive ROI if done well.

Social media posts: Free posting on Facebook pages used to have an acceptable organic reach, but recently, the platform has been more of a pay-to-play model. Many non-patients will not see a Facebook post, so I have cut back dramatically on how much effort I put into Facebook posts. It is helpful as a small secondary website because many patients will look at social media when deciding whether to call your practice.

Word of mouth: most dentists' favorite form of marketing. This is because when a patient comes in through a word-of-mouth referral, some of the trust and confidence from the previous patient transfers to the new one. Word of mouth is a great form of internal marketing, but the zone of influence (discussed later) can be very limited.

Referral from other doctors: This only applies if you have services that make sense for other dentists to refer to you, but this is the strongest form of marketing. This is because you will know a few important things if the patient is referred to you:

1. They need treatment.
2. The treatment is outside the scope of the other dentist.
3. Few other dentists can do this type of treatment in your area (supply and demand).
4. The patient starts with more trust in you because a trusted source is referring them to you.

Website: I am sure you have a website, but how well do you convert patients to make a call? Like the rest of the theory of constraints, the website can be your bottleneck. If you are attracting leads through your external marketing, but they do not take any action after they reach your web pages, you will want to work on increasing your website conversion rate.

Funnel: This is a mini-website with a clearly defined path for the user. On your website, we want a patient to go to the contact page and contact your office as soon as possible. The patient could go anywhere on the website and not take the action we want. You will use marketing to attract potential patients to a funnel, such as a free download or offer in return for providing their contact information. Your funnel progressively pushes them from a small ask, such as for an email address, to a larger one, such as to call and make an appointment or deposit for treatment. What makes the funnel special is that the landing pages are designed so the potential patient can either move forward in the funnel or stop; no other links on the landing page can distract them from the desired action.

Collecting some contact information is very important. You aim to follow up and convert them from a lead to a patient.

CRM (Customer Relationship Manager): software that tracks potential patients after they become leads. It is a great way to ensure you follow up with a lead until they become patients. After they become a patient, they are moved to your scheduling software.

Key Marketing Concepts

Zone of Influence

Each person entering your office has a zone of influence. This is the circle of friends, family, and colleagues they interact with, many of whom are potential new patients for your practice. It is common for one person to have a largely overlapped friend group with others. This is one of the significant limits of internal marketing because each person comes with a zone of influence around them. Still, if they are all referring people who are already patients, your office will not grow. This is why external marketing is so important. You need to attract new people with new zones of influence, broadening the circle of people who could be referred to you.

You always want to push your internal marketing, but I like to see internal marketing as a method of increasing the effectiveness of my external marketing.

Value Ladder

This concept is about starting with a small ask and then progressively making bigger ones. It works well because you are keeping the barrier to entry low, and you are only making a bigger ask once you have already proven yourself.

You can think of this as similar to a marriage proposal. If you ask someone to marry you on the first date, you will most likely not be successful. But if you have dated for six months and had multiple positive interactions, growing closer as you prepare for the big proposal, your chances of success get much higher.

As you move up the value ladder, your services will typically be at a higher price point and have higher profit margins. For example, you could offer a new cash patient a $99 new patient special that includes exams, x-rays, and a 1-hour time commitment. After the exam, you have had time to understand the patient's wants and needs, and you offer your monthly in-office membership plan for $34 a month. If you offered this before the exam, they likely would not agree to the monthly payments when they don't know what to expect from your office. The patient wants to test drive before they agree to buy.

During the exam, the patient informs you that they want the chip in their front tooth fixed and straighter teeth. Now that we understand their wants and needs, we can create a treatment plan connecting their desired future state with your services. You offer to crown #8 and then set up an appointment to start clear aligners.

Presenting a large treatment plan to a patient who does not understand the full value of your offer can feel like climbing up a brick wall. But after you have demonstrated your confidence and connected your services to their desired future state, that wall will look much more like a staircase.

Double Thank You

As we've discussed, we all love to buy but hate to be sold. Either way, a transaction still takes place, so what is the difference? We feel sold when we don't feel we receive sufficient value for what we spend.

You might have noticed that when you buy a cup of coffee, you and the person handing you the coffee both say thank you. Why? Because each of us is happier with what we have at the end of the transaction compared to where we started. I would rather have the coffee, and the cafe owner would rather have my money. I have gained more value from the coffee than what the money means to me. This is what needs to happen with a double thank you.

We have all had an emergency patient in horrible pain and extracted the tooth in 15 minutes. After this appointment, the patient gladly handed over their money for payment. They are so grateful to be out of pain and say thank you a hundred times. On my end, I am happy to have the production, and I thank them for coming in. We are both clearly better off after this transaction.

Some people falsely believe that business is a zero-sum game- that if I gain, you must lose. If you give me $100, you are now $100 poorer. In a mutually beneficial exchange, you receive something you value more than the $100 you pay to me. The dollars are just a component of the exchange; the important thing we are exchanging is value. Value is highly subjective and specific to every person and their situation. If you read this book and gain value, am I poorer? Did you take something from me?

Let's consider another example to illustrate this crucial concept. If I offered to sell you a gallon of water in your home for $1, you would likely not accept. You are not very thirsty, and you have many other options for water. On the other hand, if you just finished a marathon, and I offered you the same water for $10, you would likely accept because it is more valuable to you at the time. In a more extreme example, if I offered you this same gallon of water as you lay dying in the desert, you would pay me everything you had to get it. Value is based on urgency, desire, and the transformation the product or service will achieve for the person.

How much is a gallon of water worth when your basement is flooded? This water is damaging your walls, flooring, and electrical. This water has a negative value in this scenario. You would pay someone a large sum of money to remove the water.

Water has the same chemical structure, weight, and other characteristics in all these situations. But its value is determined based on the location and how it intersects with other aspects of your life.

Price Line Principle

As business owners, we look at our prices based on the cost of delivering a service: time, labor, and material. This will show us our profit margin. But a patient doesn't care about these things; they care about how much it will cost them in time, stress, and money to achieve their goals. The place where these two ideas meet is your prices.

Even though the prices are the same from both sides, your cost structures are very different. As the owner, your costs are time and material, while for the patient, it is their time, money, stress, and discomfort. As business owners, we over-stress our cost to provide a service and think the patient is looking at it the same way when they are using very different criteria to determine if there is sufficient value for their cost.

For example, a patient with severe anxiety has a higher emotional cost for dental treatment. They would be more than happy to pay the additional out-of-pocket cost to be sedated for treatment and lower their emotional cost of being scared. A patient coming in for a cleaning that is covered by insurance has no financial cost to come in and a small time cost for the appointment. If you go out of network, the patient now has the same time cost, but their out-of-pocket goes from zero to, let's say, $50. Now, they need to decide if the cost is worth the value.

Cost can come in many forms: money, time, stress, and risk. Money is the most overused and obvious: the more the patient must pay, the greater their cost.

Time is another common cost. Why do you think your patient comes to you and not another dentist three hours away? Time cost. No one wants to drive a whole day to get their dental work done. This time can be seen in the number of appointments needed to complete the work. If you can reduce the time the patient has to wait for the benefits dentistry provides, you will have reduced their time cost.

Stress is another important cost; most patients don't want to come in and get dental work. For most people, lying on your back for an hour with your mouth open is uncomfortable. On top of that, many patients fear going to the dentist. If you can reduce the stress cost to your patient, your services' value will also increase.

Risk is a cost because the patient gambles on the probability that you will reach their desired outcome. If you were going to have heart surgery to save your life, would you want the cheapest or best surgeon? If one surgeon could confidently promise you a 99.9% success rate for one price, and another would only give you an 80% success rate for half that price, which would you choose? You would choose the more expensive option; the risk of an unsuccessful operation is so high that an increase in success probability is incredibly significant. Why are people willing to pay more for a specialist to do the work? They assume the specialist will be faster and able to treat more complicated situations with a better probability of success.

Core Emotional Drives

Value is very subjective to each patient and their specific emotional state at the moment. We need to determine what the patient values. In life, we might make a logical decision, but logic will not result in action; emotion will. The pride of accomplishment drives success. The guilt we would feel from lying makes us tell the truth. Logic should help us choose the direction, but emotion is what will drive us to take action.

You might not feel this applies to you. This book is supposed to be about increasing profitability and making more money. But ask yourself *why you want this money*. Do you want the pride and status of being a successful dentist? Do you want to eliminate your debt so you can be free of stress and worry? Do you want to provide a stable future for your family? Money itself is only a tool to achieve these goals. The emotional responses that are triggered are what drive you to action.

As dentists, we are trained to focus excessively on small details to get the best results. This makes us good at our work and get amazing patient results--but the patient is buying the results, not the details. They are buying the transformation the details can achieve.

We need to discuss the benefits to the patient that the features of our services create. The patient does not want a crown with the best cement that chemically bonds to dentin; she wants a crown that she can feel confident will stay on.

Price Anchoring

A price anchor sets an expectation, even if the full price is rarely paid. People habitually focus on the first price they see as a reference point. You see this all the time with sales. The shoes you want are $200 but are marked 50% off, so you only pay $100. The seller could have sold these shoes for $100, but starting your expectations at $200 and offering them for $100 makes consumers feel like this is a good deal.

Stores like Costco use another, more clever method. These stores will have large, big-ticket items like flat-screen TVs in the front as you come in. You see this high price first, making all other prices seem much lower. If they omitted these high-priced items from the entrance, you would only compare prices to other nearby items in the store.

This strategy is easy to apply when presenting a treatment plan. First, you want to present the full fee even if the patient has insurance. This will act as your price anchor. Then, subtract the expected insurance payment or in-network insurance adjustment to reduce the price further. This will look much like the shoe example listed above.

You should discuss financing options once you have the final expected price. I prefer to have the patient pay me directly, but third-party financing is a good option if that is not feasible. In this case, we want to break the payment into monthly payments. Most people think about their budget month-to-month because most bills are paid monthly; this makes it easy for the patient to see if they can work this into their budget.

As we discussed in the chapter on Bottleneck 3: Treatment Plan Creation, you can help patients see the long-term benefits of your services in comparison to their short-term luxury expenditures; giving up eating out once a month to get a new crown is a clear, relatable swap that helps them understand the value that you offer.

Filtering Tools

In general, you want to reduce friction between when a patient starts seeking your services and when you provide those services. But in some cases, some friction or barrier to entry can be helpful.

For example, I do not recommend offering free consultations or exams to new patients. On its surface, this seems like a good idea to attract many new patients, but it can cause more problems than you might realize. First, because the patient is not paying, they may not take the appointment seriously and can no-show you without worrying about repercussions. The lost time costs you money. Second, your prices send a signal about your value. Just like a high price provides a high anchor point for future lower prices to look better, a low anchor price, like a free consult, makes all your other services look more expensive. Using some barrier to entry, such as a $99 new patient special, you are still offering a deal but filtering out people only seeking free treatment.

I have seen a similar problem with online scheduling software. I used a popular online scheduling software when I first opened my office; it seemed like a great idea for new patients to be able to schedule 24/7. But most of these patients would not show, or if they did come, they would only have Medicaid (insurance we did not accept). We would set the appointment and get ready for the patient, but when they came in and found out we could not take their insurance, they would angrily leave.

Finding the Effectiveness of Your Marketing

Now that we have defined some of our methods of marketing and selling, our goal is to reduce the cost of an acceptable treatment plan. Discussing costs includes all discounts, adjustments, or financing charges to make the treatment plan acceptable.

We want to look at all our methods of attracting patients and determine the most cost-effective ones. Insurance participation is effective at attracting and retaining patients, but it is also extremely expensive if your insurance write-off is a cost.

You should aim to reduce the average cost to generate $1,000 in acceptable treatment plan value. This could mean dropping a PPO to decrease the insurance adjustment while increasing your monthly spending on Google PPC. Your upfront cost increases slightly, but your insurance adjustment cost will decrease. All marketing will work to attract some attention to your practice, but the real question is: What is the most effective way to attract a sufficient amount of new treatment plans to your office?

Steps to Dropping a PPO Safely

1. Make Sure You Have a Treatment Plan Surplus

Remember, when you drop a PPO, you are just closing a marketing and sales channel. Before you do this, ensure you have a production surplus to keep you busy. You want to have a scheduling bottleneck.

2. Identify All In-Network Insurance Plans and Connected Umbrella or Leased Plans

This might seem simple, but understanding how you are in-network with each insurance company can be complicated. Some plans will lease out to other insurance companies, so you are in the network under both. For example, if you are in network with Cigna, that might lease to United Concordia, so you are also in network with United Concordia. This is important for a few reasons. First, you might want to drop a plan but can't directly drop it because it is part of a leased or umbrella plan.

Second, you want to know which ones are connected so you can project the total expected impact on your office when you drop a plan. You might drop a plan representing 10% of your production but then find out it is connected with several other plans, and you are dropping out of 25% of your production base. Having to drop these plans is not terrible, but you want to know what impact it will have on your practice.

3. Determine the Percent Production of Each Plan

This will help you determine the impact on your office. I prefer to focus on something other than patient head count because that can be misleading. Production will turn into your collection and profitability. You could have one plan that attracts a patient base with a lot of need and another that is only for a prophy.

4. Select Your Drop Plan

Firstly, I prefer to identify which option offers the least payment for every dollar produced. By following this method, you can boost your overall earnings without increasing production. Secondly, it's important to note any special considerations. For instance, if I stop a plan, will they send the payment directly to the patient instead? This could result in patients leaving, as many may not wish to pay for their treatment upfront.

5. Set a Date

The ideal date and how much time you need to drop a plan will be determined by the plan size and whether there are any restrictions in the insurance agreement. It is not an uncommon requirement to need to give patients at least 90 days' notice that you are dropping their plan. Another important factor is plan size. If you drop a plan representing 0.5% of production, you might be able to drop it and not experience any impact on your business, but if a plan represents 25% of total production, you will need some additional planning.

At this juncture, you want to ensure you have a sufficient surplus of treatment plans to help compensate for potential loss of production. You will most likely not lose 100% of plan patients unless they have Medicaid or a Medicare Advantage plan. I usually plan to lose about half of the patients but typically keep around 80%. It is also important to remember that if you lose half your patients but have been writing off 50% of your fee, you are still collecting the same total amount. Later, we will discuss patient retention and treatment plan replacement strategies.

6. Inform Patients That You Are Dropping Their Insurance

We need to inform our patients that the office will be dropping their insurance before contacting the insurance company. Prioritize communicating with your patients during this time and helping them understand your reasons for moving out of network. Your primary focus should be providing a positive patient experience and treatment outcome. For example, you are unwilling to shorten appointment times or double-book patients just to make this insurance adjustment make sense. Or you are unwilling to shift to a lower-quality lab or dental materials to make the numbers work. We seek to provide high-quality dentistry in a way that makes the patient feel seen and heard at their appointment.

I have provided a template letter for you if you'd like, but no magic letter will keep a patient who wants to see an in-network dentist and does not recognize your value.

Dear [name] Family,

After much deliberation, we have decided to end our preferred provider status with [dental insurance company], effective [date]. We will continue to accept your insurance. However, we will do so as an out-of-network provider.

Unfortunately, being a participating provider for [Insurance company] insurance is becoming more challenging for us as they significantly reduce our fees, sometimes by 40% or more. We have always maintained a high standard of care for our patients and have been unwilling to compromise or cut corners. This would include shifting to lower quality dental labs or shortening appointments to make these plans economically viable.

You can continue to receive your dental care at our office. With some insurance plans, there is very little difference between in-network and out-of-network benefits. However, you must read your specific insurance contract to determine if your benefits will change by going to an out-of-network provider. Feel free to call our office so that we can review your particular plan with you.

As we have begun letting patients know about the change in our status, we have found that most of our patients have chosen to pay a little more co-pay to keep the high level of care we provide. We would love the opportunity to review your plan with you and ensure you fully understand how this might or might not impact you. We are also available to discuss your specific treatment plan if you are still in the middle of completing your outstanding treatment.

We appreciate your loyalty and hope that this has only a positive impact on your dental care. Please call our office at XXX-XXX-XXXX if you have any questions about your benefits.

Sincerely,

Dr. [Name]

7. Contact the Insurance Company About Dropping Their Plan

Insurance companies do not make this easy. You may need to contact them multiple times. I would also suggest getting everything in writing in case the insurance company "loses" some documents. I believe this is a tactic they use to stall and stretch out our insurance participation a little longer.

In some cases, the insurance company will offer a better fee schedule when you go to drop them. If this new fee schedule increases the reimbursement significantly, consider staying in the network and dropping a different plan; then reach out to the patients and tell them you will remain in network. Most of the time, however, the amount they are willing to change the fee schedule is not worth the headache.

8. Keep a Close Eye on Your Schedule

You have already done all the leg work, so dropping an insurance plan should have little to no negative impact on your office. I like to let the dust settle after dropping a plan to see how the schedule is affected. There is a fair amount of work for your front desk team to reach out to all the patients, so don't jump into dropping another plan immediately. This is a good time to consider increasing your marketing spend to help compensate for any holes in the schedule.

Losing Patients When You Drop a Plan

If you are married, you likely did not find your spouse without some breakups along the way; those heartaches were necessary steps for you to learn, grow, and make room for new and better opportunities in your life.

When dropping a PPO, one of the dentists' most prominent fears is losing patients. The unfortunate reality is YOU WILL LOSE PATIENTS, at least a percentage of them.

Even with all the economic arguments and preparation, some doctors are still very scared to start dropping PPOs. They don't want to have uncomfortable conversations with patients or to see patients asking for their records to be sent to another office.

You want to avoid breaking up with a patient over your PPO status, so you stay in a PPO relationship; that way, the patient will be "loyal" to your office. But are they loyal? **If a patient only came to me because I am in network, are they a patient of my office, or are they a patient of the insurance company?**

The patient might like my office and feel we have great customer service, but in the end, if they leave my practice immediately over our insurance participation, it's clear that my office being in network was the only important factor to them.

True loyalty and connection in a relationship come from internal factors. If your partner loves you for your wit or charm, those are attached to you directly. If they are with you for an external factor like your nice car, if the car leaves, the "loyalty" leaves with it.

I get it. This can be hard to hear. The patient might have been coming to you for ten years. They bake you cookies for Christmas and keep you updated about their grandkids. But if the patient leaves when you go out of network, you ultimately know their top priority. They loved that you undervalued your skills and ability and have stayed with you because they could take advantage of you, not because of your true worth.

Sample Game Plan

This is a breakdown of my personal PPO distribution a while ago. I removed the names of insurance companies, but all the information in this chapter is based on real insurance participation situations.

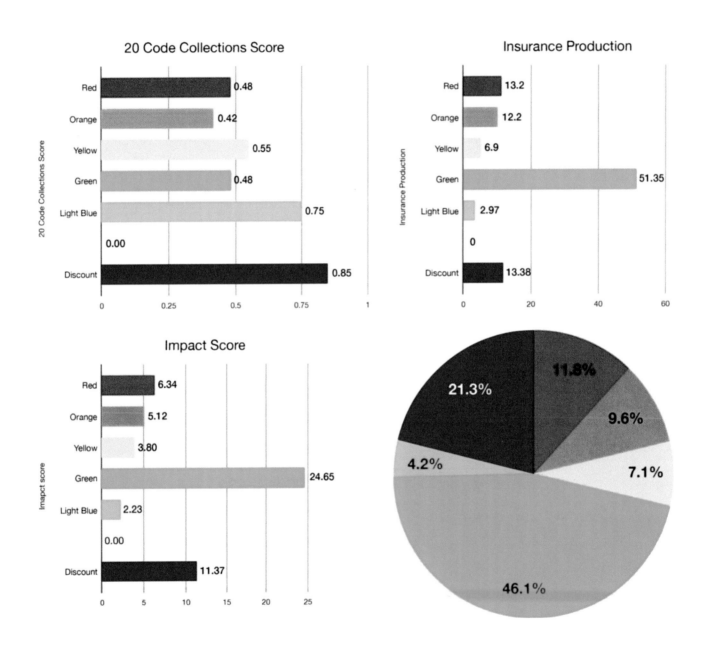

The collection score is the average amount of collection you get per dollar of production from specific insurance. This is calculated by taking your top 20 codes and comparing the fee and unit produced against your full fee schedule. For example, for Orange Insurance, we collected 42 cents for every dollar of production. This means, on average, we were writing off 58 cents for every dollar of production. The "Discount" is for my cash patient who is on my membership plan, and they receive a 15% discount on all services. In this situation, for every dollar produced, I collect 85 cents.

The insurance production score is the percent of production each insurance plan represents. For example, if a plan represents 10% of our total production, then 10 cents of every dollar produced is from that plan. This does not mean that 10% of our collections come from this plan. Our percent collections would also depend on how large the write-off is.

The impact score is created by multiplying the collections score by the percent production. This value helps give an idea of how much each insurance plan affects our total collections. For example, Orange Insurance Company is paying less per dollar of production than Yellow, but because Orange represents a larger slice of production, it has a larger impact on collections and a high impact score.

The pie chart shows how much each impact score represents as a percentage. This will give you a good estimate of how much each of these plans could impact your collections. For example, you might have two insurance company groups representing a similar percentage of production. Red represents 13.2% of production, and the Discount plan represents 13.38% of production. By contrast, the Red Insurance Company only represents 11.8% of the impact (an estimate of collections), but the Discount plan represents 21.3% of the total impact. This is because the write-offs for the Discount plan are much less than for the Red plan.

How to Use This Information

Your initial impulse might be to eliminate the plan with the largest insurance adjustment. However, a significant adjustment could result, either from a low fee schedule or because the plan constitutes a significant portion of your production. If you let go of a plan with a beneficial fee schedule and then bring in more patients on a lesser fee schedule, it could reduce your overall collections. Instead, pinpoint which fee schedules are least favorable and gradually phase out the least beneficial plans, it will systematically reduce your insurance adjustment. Start with plans that have the lowest 20 Code Collections Score.

There are also strategies to optimize participation. Take the Light Blue plan, for example. It's an umbrella plan. If you can shift external plans under this umbrella, you should receive a better fee schedule. Using this strategy, the Orange plan can be moved under the Light Blue umbrella, resulting in all Orange plan production being paid according to the Light Blue fee schedule. Consequently, the 20 code collections score would rise from 0.42 to 0.75, potentially boosting collections by 75.6% for the Orange Insurance plan without any patient loss.

You can further optimize by partially dropping some plans. Many insurances offer multiple participation tiers with varied fee schedules. Take the Green plan as an illustration: it has two tiers. The PPO pays at a 20 code collection score of 0.48, whereas a higher tier pays at 0.68. Even though there may be a patient loss with the higher fee schedule, the increased fees offset the drop in patient volume. Moreover, a decrease in patient volume means the production percentage will reduce, easing the decision to drop the plan eventually.

Despite these modifications, the Red plan remains at the bottom with a 20 Code Collections Score of 0.48. I attempted to negotiate with the company to no avail. They do offer multiple participation tiers, but the fee schedule difference is marginal. Given my packed schedule, I'm inclined to drop this plan.

Update After This Transition

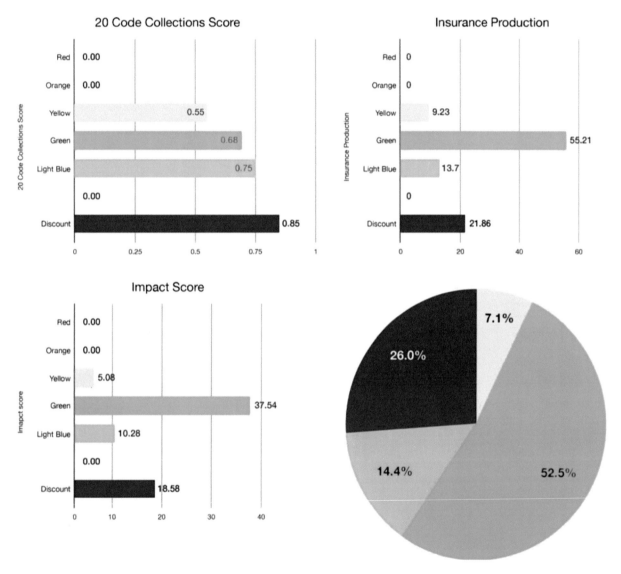

The chart depicts the revised insurance participation distribution after I started dropping the lowest-paying plans. My initial average collection score was 0.535. With the changes, it's surged to 0.714, signifying that I can collect just over 71 cents per dollar of production - a growth of 33.5%.

To put this in perspective: for a production worth $1,000,000, I used to collect $535,000. With the revamped participation structure, the collection would be $710,000. **That's a $175,000 boost without additional dental procedures!** If there were a drop in collection production, it would need to fall to $749,299.72 before I'd see a dip in collections. This dramatic shift wasn't due to dropping all plans and going fully fee for service; it was the result of dropping one and refining two.

One point of concern is that my production percentage with the Green Insurance plan has risen. This could make it challenging to drop the plan later. However, the benefits from these insurance participation changes overshadow this minor potential drawback.

These adjustments to insurance participation have also alleviated my scheduling issues. I'd consider ramping up marketing to acquire a patient surplus, leading to a new scheduling bottleneck, and then safely phase out another plan. The next plan on the chopping block would be the Yellow Insurance, given its low 20 code collections score and minimal production percentage.

Dropping Larger Plans

Dropping a larger plan can be particularly scary. There are ways to reduce or spread out the impact of dropping a large plan.

1. Do a partial drop

Many plans have different levels of participation. The most well-known one is Delta Dental, with a PPO and Premier status. The PPO pays on a lower fee schedule, but more patients have PPO insurance, and Premier has a higher fee schedule. In some cases (this is not allowed in some states), if you want to drop Delta Dental, you can drop the PPO and become a Premier Provider. This would make some of your PPO patients have a larger co-pay, but you could still accept their insurance, while patients with premier insurance would be fine. Unfortunately, this will cause a lot of confusion with your PPO patients and require your front desk to do more research when trying to estimate co-pay.

Many other insurance companies have similar setups with multiple levels of participation with different fee schedules. You can drop out of the lower-paying portions of a plan. However, some plans have connected levels, so if you drop one, you will need to drop them all. A common example is Medicare Advantage plans, which typically pay much less than the regular PPO plans and have a very low annual maximum ($500). You will be forced to accept the lower fee schedule, and the insurance will pay for very little of the treatment.

I would be very careful when doing partial drops because it creates confusion and could lead to negative reviews and bad word of mouth. However, if you have a very large plan (over 20% of total production), a partial drop can reduce your dependency on one specific plan and decrease the shock to your schedule when you fully drop.

2. Create a MASSIVE surpluses of treatment plans

If you are booking out for a year and cannot get a new patient in for even a quick consult, dropping a large plan should not affect your schedule. If your office is scheduled way above capacity, it will not feel any less busy being booked out for three months instead of 12.

You can work to have massive treatment plan surpluses by investing heavily in marketing and pre-blocking time for new patients.

Remember, you can increase your rate of treatment plan formation by adding procedures that generate larger average treatment plan values from the same number of patients. This can also have an impact because you can start offering these new services to existing patients. Tapping into your existing patient base could open up an untapped opportunity in your practice.

3. Reduce your overhead

If dropping a larger plan means a loss in production, you could see a short-term decrease in collections. If you decrease your monthly overhead, like debt payments, beforehand, this short-term loss will not feel as dramatic.

4. Give yourself a big runway

The runway is additional capital or savings you have set aside for a rainy day. If you have enough in the bank to cover all your expenses for a few months, you can tolerate a loss in collections without stressing about paying your bills.

Please note that when I talk about a runway, I am not talking about a line of credit. I am talking about liquid assets that are in a stable account.

5. PPO Optimization

This seems silly: insurance companies will not negotiate but sometimes pay you more if you are under an umbrella plan with a higher fee schedule. If you went out of network with XYZ insurance but went in with ABC umbrella with a higher fee schedule, you can stay in network with XYZ while getting paid more. Although I want you to push to drop out of as many PPOs as safely as possible, this process could take time, and it might make sense to stay in network with a plan for a little longer if it means you'll get paid more.

All my PPOs are on my drop list. The only thing that changes is the date and order I plan on doing it. If the new fee schedule is much higher than a large PPO you are afraid to drop, keeping this PPO with a new fee schedule can be a good strategic move because it increases your flexibility to drop the larger PPO.

6. Calculate collections per dollar of production based on your top 20 codes.

Knowing which fee schedule pays you the worst is one of the most important factors in determining which plan you should drop first. You should be careful not to just look at one fee. I have found some insurance companies that give you a good fee for crown and bridge but a much lower fee for everything else. They hope the dentist will be lazy and just look at the crown fee. I like to look at my top 20 most productive codes and how many units of these codes I am walking out. You might be surprised which codes impact your total production most.

To do this, you must look at your total production and select the 20 highest production codes. You must enter this into a spreadsheet with codes, descriptions, units produced, your full fee, and the insurance company fee. You can then find the total production from these fees to determine how many pennies you keep on the dollar.

If you are interested, I can create a full PPO Drop Plan for you, including a complete breakdown of your top 20 codes and a plan of action to go out of network without going out of your mind. Check out Raising Dental Income. This site is for dentists and office managers who are looking to drop some PPOs but would like extra support.

www.RaisingDentalIncome.com

7. Go in-network with small plans.

I don't prefer this tactic, but sometimes it can make sense. For example, let's say your production is 80% Delta Dental. Even a partial drop and going to premier-only status could cause you to lose too much production and be unable to cover your expenses.

Consider going in-network with a PPO if the pay is better than or equal to your current PPO participation. This, unfortunately, would mean that the patients you already see as an out-of-network provider for this plan will now be in-network, and you could see a decrease in collections from those patients.

Negotiating Fee Schedule

When you start dropping a plan, sometimes the insurance company will suddenly want to negotiate fees with you. You want to be careful with this situation because I have seen insurance companies use some sneaky tactics.

1. Make sure the fee schedule is higher than yours. An insurance company may increase some fees and decrease others. They might also increase a fee you use sparingly but decrease the fees you bill for a lot.

2. Don't accept the first fee schedule they offer. Remember, if you feel ready to drop a plan, the new fee schedule needs to be high enough that it's worth staying in the network. Wait and see if they offer you a second fee schedule that is better than the first.

3. Pay close attention to each offered fee schedule. When an insurance company sends you more than one fee schedule, one will often have the crowns paid much higher but only slightly increase your other fees. Then the other will increase all the fees evenly. The first fee schedule with the higher crown fee will have a smaller increase overall.

Membership Plans

Implementing a membership is excellent for keeping cash patients at the office. You lower your percentage of PPO patients if you have more cash patients. As you increase the number of cash or membership patients, you can more safely drop PPOs without hurting your production number.

Many people overcomplicate the creation of a membership plan. I have only one plan, which makes keeping track of the members much easier.

Thanks to dental insurance, most patients expect not to have to pay for a cleaning. I would suggest you set up your membership so a patient does not need to "pay" for their cleaning—the membership fee accounts for the cost of cleaning.

We can make the membership fee high enough to cover the fees related to standard cleaning. On average, a patient does not come in every six months for a cleaning. Precisely six months out might sit on a holiday, or your availability might not fit their schedule. Additionally, many patients will call to reschedule their appointment further out. For my calculation, I assume a patient comes in for a cleaning every seven months on average, so you will see the patient 8.57 times over five years.

In this period, you will walk out some standard codes.

D1110 (prophy) will be billed out 8.57 times

D0120 (periodic exam) will be billed out 7.57 times

D0150 (comp exam) will be billed out 1 time

D0274 (4 BWX) will be billed out 4 times

D0330 (pano) will be billed out 1 time

You can modify these numbers based on your specific office, but this is a typical setup for many offices.

I will use the fees for my zip code (24012) at the 50% level.

D1110: $95

D0120: $56

D0150: $92

D0210: $154

D0274: $74

D0330: $133

Using the above frequency, you would collect $1,913.07 over five years. Five years is equal to 60 months. You would make the same amount if you collected $31.89 a month. You can use this as a baseline for setting your membership fees based on what is included.

Some of you might feel uncomfortable charging a patient a monthly fee even if they do not use a service or come into your office. It is important to realize that when a patient has dental insurance and does not use it, the same monthly fee is charged; the patient's employer may pay it so the patient does not notice, but that fee is charged monthly regardless. Therefore, a dentist should not feel guilty about this arrangement.

Setting Your Discount Percentage

Many patients expect a discount on treatment if they sign up for a membership. I have seen this discount percentage range from 5% to 30%. Some offices change the discount percentage based on the service type, which complicates the process. Choose a set discount percentage (I use 15%) for all non-included services. If that is too steep a discount, you can raise your fee for specific services so the discounted fee sits at a level you are comfortable with.

If you think this is psychological manipulation, you are correct. Almost all of sales play this game. It's no different than when you go to the store and buy shoes for $100 because they are 50% off. You feel like you are getting a deal, but the retailer could have set the price at $100 to start with—you would pay the same, but you wouldn't feel like you got a great deal.

By having more patients on a membership plan, you can maintain control of your fee schedule. You do not need to negotiate with an insurance company to try to raise fees. When costs go up, you can raise your fees to keep pace.

Setting Your Fees

The best way to set your fee is from a fee report. A fee report is an analysis of fees in your zip code. The 50% fee is the average for your area. If you set your fee at the 80% mark, 80% of dentists in the zip codes have fees below you, and 20% have higher fees than you. Sometimes, the difference between the lowest to highest fee might be only a few dollars. In other cases, it can be a huge difference.

There are many sources for the fee report, and you will most likely need to pay a few hundred dollars for one. It might seem like a lot for a spreadsheet of fees, but if your fees are on the low side and you raise a few, it can easily pay for itself.

Increasing your fees is the fastest and simplest way to increase your profitability. If you are heavily in network with PPOs, you might feel this is useless, but it is quite valuable for a few reasons. First, it will give you a more accurate view of how much money you and your colleagues are writing off with plans. If you keep your fees lower than average, you will have a false view of how much being in network truly costs you.

Another surprising reason to raise your fees is to help negotiate the PPO fee schedule. If you submit a low fee and try to negotiate with an insurance company, that low fee will be their baseline. If you have a higher fee, you will have more negotiating power. You want to make sure your fees are above your highest PPO reimbursement. If you submit a lower fee, the insurance company will only pay up to your fee, not the negotiated maximum.

I set my fees to the 80% mark for my zip code. I update once a year between Christmas and New Year. At the very least, I would set your fees at the 50% level for your area. Never undervalue your services.

Internalized Messages

As a firm proponent of creating systems and frameworks to guide our behaviors, I hold a concept dear to my heart called "internalized messages." These are subconscious thoughts that fuel our conscious actions. Identifying these can be challenging, as they're deeply rooted in our subconscious, yet their external influence can substantially shape how we form our plans of action.

This might sound abstract or vague, but it's quite intuitive. Take, for example, someone who has earned a Ph.D. This degree confirms several things. First, the person has devoted roughly eight years to education and has presented and defended their research. They've resolved countless issues in their field and hopefully have mastered their chosen subjects.

Curious about what "Ph.D." stands for? It's a doctorate in philosophy. So, a Ph.D. in a subject indicates that the person comprehends the philosophy of that field, which could span a vast array of subjects. If someone has a Ph.D. in Psychology, they should exhibit the thought process of a Psychologist. Likewise, a Ph.D. in Mathematics should be able to think like a mathematician. After years of rigorous training, these individuals have internalized their fields' core concepts and can utilize them in future projects.

This is the essence of internalized messages. A person who has absorbed the fundamental concepts of a subject can intuitively discuss it through their mental filter. It's challenging for them to express these ideas in ways that don't align with their mental construct. We've all experienced situations where individuals interpret the same event differently due to our unique past experiences, internal filters, and internalized messages, leading to varied perceptions of identical occurrences.

The reality is that there's only one accurate description of any event. However, because of our limited and biased perceptions, we only experience a fraction of what's truly presented to us. It's as though we're only seeing a small slice of a much larger pie.

I hope this philosophical digression hasn't lost you, as this concept also ties back to the central topics of this book. I aim to help you initiate a positive shift in practice. The most significant obstacles to success are not your manual skills, marketing efforts, or location but the restrictive beliefs you harbor within.

For instance, if you started your career in a Medicaid clinic immediately after dental school, where patients were treated in high volume, you may have picked up some speed but will still need to enhance your skills or learn to present treatment plans better. This experience might have led you to label yourself a "Medicaid dentist."

Due to scheduling constraints, you may have started in a busy corporate office, where you were expected to complete a crown procedure in 45 minutes. Rushing from one patient to the next, you might have identified yourself as a "PPO dentist."

Meanwhile, on social media, you see a show-off dentist performing extensive procedures, making more money in one day than you do in a month. Looking at their success, you think, "I could never be that guy."

Labels like "Medicaid dentist," "PPO dentist," or "I could never be that guy" are all examples of internalized messages. They are narratives we tell ourselves that shape our thoughts and behaviors. It's essential to take a step back sometimes and examine our actions and thoughts and the reasons behind them. More often than not, we are holding ourselves back, not the world around us.

Venturing outside our comfort zone can be daunting, but sometimes, it's precisely where we should be.

Mindset, Leadership, and Culture

Certain terminology often circulates within dental and business circles, sounding impressive but lacking tangible significance. "mindset," "leadership," and "culture" are three such terms. Pose a question regarding these terms to ten dentists, and you'll likely receive ten different explanations. Undoubtedly, these concepts carry significant weight, but defining them precisely can prove challenging. The issue is further compounded when we assume a shared understanding of these words, leading to potential miscommunication. We may think we're discussing the same subject when our perspectives differ significantly.

Hence, establishing a shared understanding of these terms is paramount to me. My goal is to help dentists find fulfillment in their practice and working lives, and I'm driven by my own experiences to prevent others from facing similar struggles.

"Mindset" refers to ingrained beliefs that interpret external stimuli and guide our thoughts and actions. These beliefs aren't always consciously known; we deduce them from our reactions to stimuli. Elements of mindset include adherence to certain procedures and emotional responses to specific situations, like risk aversion. Your mindset is the total collections of internalized messages that guides your behavior.

For instance, some may say I have a "scarcity mindset" versus an "abundance mindset" when dealing with business issues in dentistry. Owning a dental practice has made me more risk-averse, prompting me to understand my financial metrics to inform my actions.

"Leadership" embodies how business owners and management enact their mindset to influence their teams. This can be achieved through personal communication or organizational policies and procedures.

Your leadership style stems from your mindset. Your interactions will reflect this positivity if you're optimistic about your proactive team. **Similarly, if you believe patients deserve care that aligns with their goals, regardless of insurance coverage, this belief will manifest in your treatment plans, policies, and patient communication.**

"Culture" encapsulates the collective mindset fostered by your leadership and policies among your staff and patients.

Culture is the enduring reflection of your leadership practices. In my office, I've communicated to my team that I want to be the dental practice patients choose rather than the one they settle for. This selection process implies that patients have other alternatives, and after consideration, they decide on my office. If I depended solely on an external source for patients, like being included in a PPO insurance list, then patients would not be choosing my practice but ending up in it.

To summarize, your mindset informs your leadership style, shaping your culture. If you're unhappy with your office culture, reflecting on the root causes is crucial. As the owner, you're ultimately responsible for your positive or negative office culture. The hiring and firing decisions, insurance involvement, chosen procedures, patient experience, and daily activities are all under your control.

Is Your Business Root Bound?

My wife loves to garden. She grows vegetables and beautiful flowers. I do not particularly enjoy the garden, but I still like to get involved in her gardening projects. One fascinating aspect is when a plant gets root bound: when a plant remains in a pot too long, the root grows in circles and forms a tight ball. At this point, even if the plant is put into high-quality soil with room to stretch out and grow in all directions, it will not embrace the new opportunity. The roots stick to their tried-and-true method of growing in a tight little spiral.

The sad part is that the plant is sometimes so ingrained in this method of "growth" that it chokes itself out of all the nutrients, trying to continue feeding off the limited volume it grew accustomed to.

You might wonder why the plant would do this to itself. In the simplest terms, this method worked for a long time. In the seedling stage in the little pot, focusing on this safe method of staying within its limits was the right thing. But as its environment changed, it failed to embrace new opportunities to grow in its new surroundings; it just kept growing inward.

What if tomorrow was different than yesterday? Your cost increased, but your insurance reimbursement never did. What if you tried to make it work? You look internally to ensure the system is more efficient and continue paying your bills with the limited nutrients in your office. You will spiral tighter and tighter each year, and even if you get better at your work, you will find it harder to stay afloat as time goes on. You'll find yourself depleted and weak, trying to survive on an ever-shrinking nutrient base.

At first, the plant is smart to make the most of the nutrients it has available in the pot. But it is foolish to keep using the same old methods when placed in a new world. Sometimes we must raise our heads and look around to see the new opportunities arising around us.

You can follow the same spiraling method that allows you to hobble along—turning your once-vibrant office into a dull, wilted mess. Or, you can learn to grow and tap into the opportunities around you. Break free from the spiral draining your remaining nutrients and tap into what the rest of the garden offers. The choice is yours. What path will you take?

Do You Need Extra Help Dropping PPOs?

Is it physically painful to see your insurance adjustment each month?

Are you feeling burnt out and overworked?

Are you ready to take action but feeling held back because you don't know where to start?

If you are ready to shift away from PPO participation with an organized, practical plan to minimize risk, scan the QR code below! You will be taken to Raising Dental Income.

www.RaisingDentalIncome.com

You will see a full breakdown of my reports and services to help you go out of network without going out of your mind.

Happy Dropping!

About the Author

Dr. Burkitt is a general dentist who launched his practice, We Care Dental Care, in 2019. Initially, he joined many PPO networks and even accepted Medicaid. As his practice matured, he delved into the financial implications of partnering with insurance networks and realized how costly it was.

With a growing family to support, Dr. Burkitt was keen on transitioning out of these insurance networks. However, he wanted to ensure a smooth and predictable transition. This quest led him to the strategies outlined in The Dropping Dental PPOs Playbook. The playbook provides a blend of detailed calculations and real-world insights, offering tactics to confidently move away from insurance affiliations without undue stress.

Outside of his professional commitments, Dr. Burkitt cherishes moments spent with his wife and daughter. He has been a notable guest on the FFS Podcast and The Dental Marketer Podcast multiple times. Furthermore, his insightful articles have sparked numerous discussions in dental-related Facebook groups.